ENEMY
NUMBER ONE

The Secrets of the UK's Most
Feared Professional Punter

Patrick Veitch

RACING POST

DISCLAIMER – the names of three individuals have been changed for reasons of security.

This papeback edition published in 2010 by Racing Post Books
Compton, Newbury, Berkshire, RG20 6NL

First published in 2009

A catalogue record for this book is available from the British Library.

ISBN 978-1-905156-70-2

Edited by Steve Dennis and Jonathan Powell

Cover designed by Adrian Morrish
Interiors designed by Tracey Scarlett

Printed in the UK by CPI Bookmarque, Croydon

CONTENTS

ACKNOWLEDGMENTS

I would like to thank my parents, John and Norma, for everything they've done for me. It must have been from them that I inherited the determination that has stood me in such good stead over the years.

I want to thank all those who helped me at the time of my departure from Cambridge, whether with advice, assistance or protection. Their help was invaluable at a critical time in my life. They know who they are. Praise must also go to the many people who have helped me in the battle with the bookmakers, notably Geoffrey Pooley and Charles 'Robot' Robarts. I would also like to express my gratitude to Steve Dennis and Jonathan Powell, who helped me to turn my very rough first manuscript into a far more polished end result.

Patrick Veitch

FOREWORD

L ET'S face it, we would all like to earn our living from backing horses but the bottom line is we either don't have the intelligence, don't work hard enough or don't have the courage. Read this book and you will understand exactly what is required to 'cut it' at the highest level. It is a fascinating insight into the mind of someone whose brain ticks a whole lot quicker and more precisely than most.

It tells of the coups that have been pulled off, the thinking behind them and the money won. It isn't boastful just fact. Logical views are given on every aspect of racing and betting and there are some wonderful insights into a number of well known trainers and jockeys. It also details the very real threat to his life, how he coped with it and how the experience changed his life forever. It's a fascinating read no matter what your background or interests and one that will undoubtedly change the way you think.

John Francome

PART ONE

EARLY DAYS AND TROUBLED TIMES

WILDEBEEST look very cool munching on their daily diet when they don't perceive any obvious threat. When the lions arrive it's really only a question of how quickly they can run away, although the most dangerous lions will often succeed in making a kill. Sometimes, when a pack of lions are particularly well organised, they will make repeated kills over a sustained period.

In this book you can read about lions and wildebeest, about me and the bookmakers. You can also read about brain surgeons, mad axemen and thunderstorms, and about the £20 million that I and my allies have taken from the bookmakers since 1999. They haven't enjoyed the last few years as much as I have, many even changing the way they operated in an attempt to stop me winning.

Over the years, I'd rely on a total of around 200 agents to place my bets. I'd learn to use what I termed 'guile accounts' to mislead the bookmakers. And, on a busy day at the races, I'd sometimes take 14 mobile phones with me. The *Racing Post* described me as 'the bookmakers' public enemy No. 1'. Others have called me Keyser Soze, after the 'man who wasn't there' in the film *The Usual Suspects*, branding me a mystical figure reputed to be behind many major gambles. I was repeatedly told that it was my business that the major firms feared the most. Not only can I hit them for a million pounds in a matter of weeks, but I exert strict control over my betting so the overall risk to my capital is very small.

Of course, I still backed many sizeable losers and had to deal with unprofitable periods that lasted as long as four months, but over the years I've made a profit of 16.7 per cent on my turnover despite having to take well under the going rate to obtain a large enough stake. Another professional punter, the big-staking Harry Findlay, has been quoted as saying that no punter on the planet wins more than eight per cent on his turnover. Although I've needed to be secretive about my location over the years, I've always been on planet Earth.

But it's not all been a high-roller's paradise. Without warning, my life was threatened and I was forced to go into hiding, changing my name, my circumstances and my location to make sure that I wasn't found. The ramifications of what happened affect me even now. For the period in which my life was turned upside down, I wanted compensation and the bookmakers were my target.

It was only by waiting for a period when I took a break from racing that it was possible to tell the full story. I'm fortunate to be in a position where I don't have to devote all my energies to taking on the bookies. A sabbatical gave me time to write the book; it also allowed me to make some key changes to the way I placed my bets and created some distance in time from the most detailed stories. This ensures that I haven't assisted the bookmakers in their obsessive desire to track my activities. I've been able to provide every detail on the key years of 1999-2004, as well as the important highlights after that.

This book is not a betting manual, but I'm sure there is enough information here to provide some guidance and plenty of information for those who wish to take their punting more seriously.

But there is one key reason for writing this book. It keeps a promise I made to myself when at my lowest ebb, in the second half of 1998. When I was right at the bottom, I told myself that I would return to racing when it was safe to do so and later tell my story, although it hasn't always been an easy task. This is the story.

CHAPTER 1

THROUGH THE DOOR

SOME people grow up knowing what they want to do; some grow old without finding their true calling. For me, the die was cast at the age of 15 on a half-holiday from school. I opened a betting shop door, and that was that.

From an early age, I loved to play cards, especially if there was the chance of finding someone willing to gamble for small stakes. Maybe my parents' choice of school contributed a little, as the one-hour coach journey there allowed plenty of time to indulge this hobby.

My parents, John and Norma, had what you might call 'proper' careers; my father is a successful businessman and mother used to teach in a primary school. They worked hard to pay the school fees for my brother Jonathan and me, and they would have expected that a good education would lead to a traditional career, probably in the financial world. Maths was my strongest subject at school, so this seemed an obvious path. There was certainly no danger of my becoming an artist, as my attempts to draw or paint were legendary among my classmates. No-one had ever seen anything quite so bad.

However, my interest in gambling skyrocketed the moment I stepped through the betting shop door. My eyes lit up with excitement. I could see odds and numbers everywhere and money changing hands. It was an adult version of playing cards for small change, a fascinating new world and one in which I was determined to become involved. Technically, I was too young, but that didn't seem to prevent all my bets being accepted – if only that was still the case today.

I'd heard that bookmakers were always supposed to win, but even at that early stage it was clear to me that the typical punter wasn't giving himself any chance of beating them. The customers in the shop gave little thought to their betting, rather showing an obsessive interest in following the race-by-race selections provided in the newspapers on display. A 15-year-old could have told them – had they been interested in listening to one – the 'strategy' was doomed from the start, as if those tips had been consistently successful the betting shop managers would not have pinned them up to begin with.

I started out with one very powerful tool: the knowledge that I didn't have the first idea how to win. A little knowledge may be a dangerous thing, but I had none whatsoever. Armed with this innocence, and feeling my way as if down a dim passageway that grew slowly brighter at each turn, I restricted my first few bets to cricket, a game on which I'd been mad keen from an early age. Although my view that England were often overrated wasn't too far wide of the mark, I couldn't help feeling that cricket was too simple a betting medium to make it profitable after deducting the dreaded betting tax that applied in betting shops until 2001. That statement may seem odd. Why, you might ask, would I not want betting to be simple? That's also simple. To win consistently, you need the odds to be wrong. In most sports, the basic abilities of the various teams are widely known. There are only a small number of easily discernible variables, such as pitch, weather and the recent form of the players.

Horseracing grabbed my attention after a short while because it was so much more complex, so much more demanding. It offered the attraction of a huge pool of horses, many of them barely known, with a lengthy list of factors that could affect their performance. I tried a few theories but was stabbing in the dark before the acquisition of a couple of form books gave me something concrete to work on. I'd spend most of my evenings neglecting my homework, instead leafing through the form books trying out all manner of ideas to see what was successful and what wasn't. In each case I'd assess the profit or loss per bet, in percentage terms, of the strategy. This may seem a little advanced for your typical novice, but I had a way with numbers and it came naturally to me to proceed in this fashion.

What happened if you backed the favourite for a place on the Tote in every race? What about just odds-on shots? What about favourites at starting price? Did they do better in handicap hurdles or novice hurdles? What about the bookmakers' bonus bets – could I combine the hottest favourites on a Saturday to give myself the best chance of landing the bonus on a Yankee or Union Jack? These were fairly naive strategies – not as naive as following newspaper tipsters race by race, though – and gradually I learned from them. They didn't show me how to win, but told me which races gave me the best and worst chances of success. Later, I'd find that there were books packed with all manner of such statistics, divided not just by course but by trainer, so that you could analyse the vital data from all angles. Trainer statistics were often interesting at particular courses, as well as when certain jockeys were used and when assessing stables that did well with horses on their first or second run of the season.

My punting became all about horseracing. I'd gone through the looking-glass and there was no going back. I'd bet on Saturdays and on Wednesday afternoons, the half-day at school. There were more than a few winners among the typical avalanche of losers, but I didn't make a profit after deducting tax, travel costs and the cost of my form books. Crucially, though, I was learning fast.

My progress on the fast track was unfortunately derailed when my father discovered some of my betting slips, and was consequently horrified. He had a working knowledge of racing, being a frequent viewer of televised action, occasional punter and visitor to racecourses himself, where his binoculars were adorned with the typical collection of pasteboard badges. He later became an owner with Peter Beaumont, but at the time he was understandably concerned that his son was being led astray. Led? I was making the running! He phoned the security manager at the local William Hill and demanded to know why they were accepting bets from someone who was underage. I was soon barred from the shop – a taste of things to come, as bookmakers have been trying to stop me betting with them ever since. There are more ways than one through the wood; I took my bets to the nearby Coral shop, and continued as before.

I was a precocious child – you may have gathered – and went to secondary school at ten instead of 11, and then gained another year along the way so that I was 14 when I started A-levels. I submitted my university application form at 15, with not a shadow of doubt that I would do Maths at Cambridge. I think you are supposed to hope to do this rather than decide, but I have to be honest and say I decided. Call it the confidence of youth, if you like, or some other less benevolent term if you must. I filled in my application form with my five choices: Cambridge, blank, blank, blank, blank.

Inevitably, I was summoned by Mr Ward, the Head of Maths, to explain myself. Asked what I would do if Cambridge turned me down, I said they'd have to accept me 12 months later. I wasn't willing to enter other options as a form of insurance as I wasn't willing to go anywhere else. We had a similar discussion about the separate Cambridge application form, because I had chosen three famous historical colleges. Once again, I refused his advice to nominate one or two newer colleges that would be less in demand from the best applicants. I must have given Mr Ward a few more grey hairs, but he was to have the last laugh. I looked nailed on for at least one of the two Maths prizes awarded in my year, but he awarded one to a boy who was going on to study engineering and decided not to award the other prize.

My confidence – or maybe that less benevolent term – was rewarded, and I left school at 16 having done A- and S-levels and with my place at Trinity College, Cambridge secured. My interview at Trinity lasted only about ten minutes, although I was told that I might have cause for optimism based on my exam scores. I was expecting this to go down very well with my parents when I returned home, but the discovery that I'd gone to a big race meeting at Doncaster after the interview and managed to lose my travel bag into the bargain meant that I was far from popular.

I didn't get to Cambridge as quickly as I'd hoped. From the day the letter arrived confirming that I'd got a place at Trinity, there was a two-year wait until I was old enough to start as an undergraduate. The rules were clear – only if my parents moved to Cambridge could I enrol sooner. Had I been a month younger it would have been a three-year wait. It was frustrating that I had to wait so long, especially as Cambridge was just 15 miles from Newmarket . . .

To provide an income, I took a job as a cashier/administrator at a building society, the best part of a dull job being the office's proximity to a betting shop. That was my lunch hour sorted, and there were also the occasional 'unavoidable' absences from my desk during the afternoons. At that stage, my betting was showing a small profit, but trips to the races, newspapers and form books whittled down that profit into a net loss. Things changed after I turned 17, as my driving instructor, Warren Nicholls, quickly became a willing partner in my betting pursuits. Soon I was having £20 to £50 on a horse without too much worry, the paper trail that winds through the lives of all punters growing with experience and audacity.

Pulled up at the side of the road, ostensibly studying the Highway Code but minds elsewhere, Warren and I devised a plan to take matters further. I would set up a tipping service, advertising in the weekly racing papers and providing my selections on an answerphone. Warren took care of the administration while I made the selections. Combining this with my day job made for a hectic lifestyle, but my racing involvement started to show a profit after expenses and I was able to increase my weekend racing trips while saving some money for university. The day I passed my test, I drove straight to the nearest racecourse for an afternoon's underage betting! At 18, I finally went up to Cambridge.

My fruitful partnership with Warren ended in my first year, as we were too far apart to work effectively together. During the summer holiday, I realised that a more effective tipping medium would be to advertise in the *Racing Post* as an 'odds to' tipster. This involved clients phoning up on the day of the race and receiving a bet in return for agreeing to pay the profit to a fixed stake, in my case £10, if the horse won. The method had a bad reputation within racing as there were plenty of con-men around, but it had the advantage to clients of being able to join on the same day as their first bet. I had to trust them to pay up, of course, but as long as enough of my bets won, clients would be keen to pay to make sure they received the next selection.

I soon earned a decent reputation and my client base increased quickly, as I was making steady profits. By March of my second year at Cambridge, I had more than 100 people phoning up for my advice. Although I advised only two or three bets a month, it still meant that I had up to £1,000 running on a horse for me each time, which was a lot for a second-year student. It was a lot for a lot of people! I was running up much larger costs in phone bills and travelling more often to the races but still making a decent profit, especially as I now had the funds to bet more heavily myself. By that stage I was playing at the £500-1,000 level when I was very keen on something.

Gambling quickly taught me the twin values of self-discipline and discretion. Any gambler worthy of the name should retain the discipline to keep records of every bet, otherwise it is human nature to remember the winners and conveniently forget the losers. That way you can kid yourself you are winning when the truth is much bleaker. The records also ensure that no money goes missing, should a bookmaker or agent make a mistake in their calculations. However, recording all bets shouldn't tempt you to dwell too much on them. You shouldn't assume that because you have been backing losers your methods are wrong. It is not black and white. You must be keenly aware that you are concentrating on a group of animals running across a field, and can't know for sure which one is going to get there first. Over a period of a week or a month, sheer chance will affect how you perform as a gambler.

Being discreet in all gambling matters is vital. At the age of five I was considered to be uncontrollable and was in no way bashful about what I said. I think I've improved a little on that score. When I started gambling, it soon became clear that the bookmaking industry relied on tip-offs to warn them when informed money was being placed. I would need to ensure that I gave no clues to anyone until I was ready to bet.

At Trinity, however, it was impossible to disguise the source of my new income. To support the business, my college room was full of phones, televisions and electrical equipment, causing one friend who called round to exclaim: "It's like Curry's in here!" The sheer number of phone calls that my tipping service produced meant that I needed someone to answer the phones for me on busy days. I'd joined the Horseracing Society as soon as I arrived at Cambridge; there were two very attractive girls among the racegoers, so when it came to recruiting telephonists they were the obvious choices. Suddenly my male friends were popping round on a regular basis to gaze adoringly at Katie Derham, now much better-known as an ITV newsreader, and her friend Kate James when they were hard at work answering the phones. I paid them £5 an hour to answer the phones for three hours each morning and pass on my selections for the day, which allowed me more time to concentrate on the form book.

My burgeoning business inevitably led to one or two problems with my tutor. All phone lines had to be registered with the college and when a routine check was made my answerphone message about next Saturday's bet was discovered. Result: stern lecture and warning about the dangers of addiction to gambling (at least the horse won). I also had to tread carefully with the college porters, as pertinent questions might have been prompted by the increasing amount of my mail. After a successful Saturday I might have 30-40 letters containing cheques on the Tuesday morning. Fortunately, Paddy the porter was a racing man and, after I'd given him one or two carefully chosen tips, he assured his colleagues that young Mr Veitch was a fine gent who should be looked after.

I went racing regularly in that second year, usually with Paul Graham, a PhD student. He had rather more commitments than me, but managed to do his university work in the evenings and frustrate anyone checking on his daytime activities by leaving a trail of notes in various locations, each one suggesting that he had now left and gone somewhere else. My interest in the Maths course had disappeared completely; after the first day of the second year, I didn't attend another lecture. I still had to survive the twice-weekly one-hour supervisions, which involved taking answers to a set problem sheet, but fortunately I had friends willing to help me.

My copying system relied on the knowledge that we had a different supervisor for each subject, changed every term, so that each supervisor would teach for a maximum of four sittings. A mystery illness (vet's certificate) would exclude me from one of these, so any supervisor had only three hours to rumble me. Supervisors were mostly research students with a pleasingly easy-going approach, so I survived the first two terms of my second year despite not understanding a single question, never mind my copied answers.

Another ploy was needed for the end-of-year exam, however,

and I was fortunate that it was possible to gain quite a bit of credit for doing a shared computer project. I clubbed together with my friend David Craggs, and to my certain benefit we managed to stretch the definition of the word 'share', as his efforts were a lot more impressive than mine. Our shared mark, combined with a week of last-minute swotting, allowed me to scrape through the second year. Other students called this last-minute work revision, but in my case it was just 'vision'.

The end-of-year social events were easier to manage. One night Marcus Armytage, who had won the Grand National on Mr Frisk that spring, becoming the last amateur to win the great race, came to talk to the Cambridge University Racing Society. Marcus, now a racing journalist, seemed surprisingly subdued when he arrived, but as the night wore on and the drink flowed, he became quite full of himself. During his speech he had a light-hearted dig at me by suggesting that strictly on drinking ability I was more of an amateur than him, and afterwards he was so boisterous that he slapped me on the shoulder and sent me off to get him another drink 'sharpish'. Naturally, I obliged. I bought him a double and kept them coming, with the result that in the last hour before his taxi arrived the hero of the Grand National was laid out cold on a bed in the recovery position.

I bumped into Marcus at Newmarket races the next day. He was much quieter, and reported that he'd had an argument with the taxi driver on the way home the previous night. He'd accused the cabbie of taking him to the wrong address, only to discover – after harsh words had been exchanged – that that wasn't the case.

Towards the end of my second year, I had a client called Dave Mitchell, who turned out to be the sports manager of Supercall, suppliers of racing commentaries and most of the clublines for the top football teams. He had made good profits from my advice and suggested that we set up a premium-rate telephone service to replace my tipping service. Nearly all the premium-rate tipsters were well-known racing personalities or journalists, but my service would be billed differently. I would be advertised as 'The Professional'.

The service launched at the beginning of my third year at Cambridge. It was an instant success, soon generating gross revenue in excess of £10,000 a month. I took on a partner, Peter Axon, to assist with the form study and obtaining of information and we worked tirelessly to produce my two daily bulletins. The first message went out at 8.30pm the night before racing, so I would be on the mobile for most of the informal sitting in the college dining hall. It raised a few eyebrows, although most people were used to it by then.

The premium-rate number took up almost all my time. In my first two years at university I'd managed to fit in occasional sporting activities, and I represented Trinity at cricket, squash, tennis and, occasionally, pool and darts. That said, when I played cricket I had to ensure that at least one friend was always among the spectators to answer my mobile and alert me if the call was urgent. Occasionally I had to feign an urgent toilet break in order to deal with the situation. Sports and studies alike went out of the window in my third year, as I dashed around the college to get anything non-racing out of the way before heading back to bury my head in the form book. One of Peter's friends labelled me 'Michael J' after the old film *The Secret of My Success*, in which Michael J Fox played a dual life as a mailboy and senior executive in the same firm.

Now and again I made it to the college bar before 10.30pm, but even that backfired one night when I bumped into John Maxse, now director of communications at the Jockey Club but then a broadcaster at Supercall. He challenged Dave the next day to explain why their professional gambler was a student at Cambridge, something Dave and I had never planned to make public. John's fears were put to rest when Dave assured him that I worked twice as hard as most non-students and that he'd extensively 'tested the goods' before signing me up.

I may have worked twice as hard as most non-students, but it was all in one direction and there was no time to devote to my finals. I managed to bluff my way through another year's supervisions but left without finishing my degree, something of an irony considering my single-minded efforts to get to Trinity in the first place. My parents were disappointed, but as my racing business took off I hoped they would understand.

CHAPTER 2

BABY-FACED ASSASSIN

M Y BUSINESS hardly changed after I left university. I rented the first flat that I viewed in Cambridge while most of my friends left town, many of them to work in the City. When I went down to London for a night out and to catch up with them, I couldn't believe how early they had to be up each morning. Many of them started work at 6.30 or 7.00 after a long commute and then toiled away well into the evening. I had to work hard, too, but I didn't have to get up before dawn. To all intents and purposes I was basically pursuing my hobby and could go racing as often as I liked.

The supply of premium-rate telephone services quickly expanded as many other tipsters jumped on the bandwagon. Eventually the market became saturated with allegedly shrewd professionals, as opposed to the handful of celebrity tipsters who had started the ball rolling a few years earlier. I would have backed my service against any of them, but inevitably the sheer volume of opposition in the market affected the business, not least because the number of opportunists produced a rather downmarket image of premium-rate tipsters.

A problem occurred when one tipster, Henry Ponsonby, launched a service called 'Best of the Rest' that was passing on the selections of other tipsters. *The Sporting Life* accepted his adverts, but other advertisers were most unhappy at the development. There were many complaints, but very little was done to sort it out. I suspected that Ponsonby, very much 'one of the boys' in my view, was being looked after by his friends at the paper.

I may have been the youngest person in the business by a mile but I wasn't standing for it. When I first contacted the Life, they failed to listen to my concerns, so I faxed them cancelling my daily adverts until further notice. The drastic action worked – within a few days the adverts for 'Best of the Rest' were stopped. However, the letter I received from editor Monty Court left me fuming. It ended: "I hope that is the end of the matter, because I have no wish to involve myself further in the hard-nosed business of selling tips." I was most unhappy about the letter, as it was his paper that allowed the problem to escalate in the first place. I gradually moved nearly all my business to the *Racing Post*, a paper I much preferred anyway.

My image remained intact within the industry, and I was regularly in demand for newspaper articles and the occasional TV appearance. I was profiled in the Saturday and Sunday Telegraph as well as in some of the tabloids, including the Sun, whose racing correspondent Claude Duval was keen for a quote for his headline to the effect that I'd take the bookmakers for a million pounds over my career. That turned out to be a somewhat unambitious target. I drew the line at the News of the World, though, and declined an interview, only to receive a call from a friend one Sunday morning to report that they'd printed a double-page spread about me anyway. They named me 'the baby-faced assassin of the betting ring'; my friends took the opportunity to call me 'BF' for some time afterwards.

At around the same time, the BBC launched 'Esther' in the style of an English version of 'Oprah' and I was asked to appear on a programme about gambling. When I arrived, there were quite a few familiar racing figures in the studio, including John McCririck along with on- and off-course bookmakers. I'd been told we would all be in the audience, but the researcher soon told me that I was one of three people up on the stage and that Esther Rantzen was starting the programme with me. Beside me on the stage were the mother and wife of addicted gamblers, which left me concerned that I had been set up for a rough ride. Perhaps I fooled them with my 'nice young man routine', but the show worked fine as it largely split into separate sections about good and bad gamblers.

The only worrying part was when one of the invited audience waved his finger wildly and informed me that all gambling was evil according to the Koran. He followed up with a warning about the inevitability of it all crashing down in a sea of addiction, which bore a remarkable similarity to the lecture given to me by my tutor at Cambridge. At least Esther did her best to fight my corner.

However, when ITV approached me, I was less impressed. They wanted to profile me and I was asked if I watched morning gallops at Newmarket. I didn't, but they liked the idea of filming me watching the gallops through my binoculars, so they insisted on having that image anyway. That should have sounded a warning note. In the interview, they asked for a bet for that day and I replied: "Actually I'm not having a bet at all today, I think it's much too difficult, but if you absolutely forced me to put my head on the block then . . ." When it was shown, this was edited to "put my head on the block . . ." and the entire piece was based around their footage from Newmarket and the fact that my 'head on the block' selection had been beaten. The whole episode reinforced my view that you shouldn't believe everything you see or read in the media.

An important development in my business came when Supercall was bought out by Ladbrokes. This wasn't exactly the image I was looking for, as the last thing I wanted was for potential clients to believe that I had a connection with the racing department at Ladbrokes. The situation was far from ideal and I wasn't happy with the new management that were handling my account. It was time to move on.

Out of the blue, I received a call from Nigel Stewart, who co-owned a tipping service called the Winning Line that had exploited a niche in the market. The Winning Line charged a large yearly subscription for their service and wanted to sign me up because Nigel's partner and chief tipster Stephen Winstanley needed a heart transplant. Winstanley had been very taken with my advice for the filly Mysilv at double-figure odds before Christmas for that year's Triumph Hurdle in March, a race she duly won. On my racing line, in the weeks before the race, I had repeatedly taunted the bookmakers about their impending losses on the filly. I was unhappy with my situation at Supercall/Ladbrokes and needed little persuasion to agree a deal. We settled on a fee of £100,000 plus bonus for the first year.

Every horse selected for the Winning Line shortened instantly in the betting, rather like they do for the Post's Pricewise column these days. In those days there wasn't a proper market on most races until the afternoon, so that the odds taken were badly affected. Still, the selections I provided in that year still showed a healthy profit, which counted towards an additional bonus. Nevertheless, I found it a very trying time. Stewart and Winstanley were keen to have a high number of selections, so a lot of the horses advised were from other tipsters on their books. Crucially, customers didn't know which selections were mine.

The Lobilio affair, in February 1995, was particularly difficult. During the winter, the service had a very good run, to the point where there was a stampede every time a selection was given out. In the previous fortnight, we'd received two separate tip-offs about foul play from sources in the betting industry, rumours that dopers were at work administering banned substances to horses to prevent them winning. On the way to the start of a handicap hurdle at Hereford, one of our selections, Lobilio, dropped dead.

This led to a media frenzy, with all the papers wanting to discuss what had happened. I even ended up on BBC News. It was annoying that in some sections of the media any suggestions of doping were dismissed as ridiculous. Doping horses to prevent them winning had been proved in the early 1990s, but it was apparently inconceivable when it came to the most heavily gambled horses of 1995, which were often Winning Line selections. Doping was again discovered in 1998, but I can't recall anyone writing a retraction.

The jump season ended well when Master Oats, who we'd tipped ante-post for the Cheltenham Gold Cup at 16-1, won the race as hot favourite, but I found the following summer very tiring. I had to deal with endless amounts of controversy created by the huge effect that our selections had on the betting market. In the circumstances I couldn't continue in such a position for much longer but, rather than quit in a blaze of publicity and further controversy, I eased my way out quietly. I did a results-based deal for the following year that allowed me to advise no horses at all if I chose. When it became clear how literally I was taking this over the next few months, we agreed to terminate the contract.

The move led to an arrangement with Michael Tabor, one of the largest and most renowned punters in modern times. Tabor, a West Ham fan who was brought up in the East End, began his working life as a trainee hairdresser but swiftly found that line of work didn't provide enough excitement for him. He started out as a bookmaker by buying two betting shops cheaply, and quickly set about extending his betting empire under the banner of Arthur Prince. He played both gamekeeper and poacher, betting to big stakes and remaining a familiar figure in the ring at places like Royal Ascot, York, Goodwood and Cheltenham.

This heady mix of business and pleasure came to an end in 1995 when he cashed in his chain of 114 Arthur Prince betting shops for a sum said to have been £28 million. He had owned racehorses for many years and had enjoyed the biggest success of his life that spring when his Thunder Gulch won the Kentucky Derby. That £28m was invested wisely, as he joined forces with John Magnier and Aidan

O'Brien in Ireland and became one of the leading owners in the world. Horses such as High Chaparral, Montjeu, Rags To Riches and Hurricane Run have won no end of major races in his famous orange and blue colours, as have many great names in which he has a share with his Ballydoyle cohorts, and he continues to pursue his hobby with great vigour.

Michael rang my home in Cambridge, but at the time I was still involved in the Winning Line so, despite an interesting chat, I was unable to commit at that stage. He is a fiery individual who knows exactly what he wants and does not hesitate to go after it, so after I left the Winning Line we made contact again and discussed coming to an agreement for Michael to receive my selections, finalising the deal over dinner at the Lygon Arms at Broadway during a Cheltenham meeting.

Michael was willing to match my salary from the Winning Line of £100,000 a year for a full year. Instead, I opted to settle for an arrangement based solely on Flat turf racing, which allowed me to take a long break during the winter to recharge my batteries, a routine I maintain to this day. I'd been equally profitable on the Flat and over jumps, but felt that I could do better still if I focused on just one code. Michael wanted me to select horses exclusively for him. It was strictly a business arrangement – we hardly ever met. He would ring me in the morning to see what I fancied, and in any one week I would probably give him four or five selections. I needed to place my own bets carefully to avoid affecting the price that Michael took, as although I was betting in fair amounts, up to around £5,000 a time, he was a much bigger player.

Such was Michael's reputation that he was only able to place substantial bets in the afternoon, so we agreed to ignore early prices. His only difficulty was in placing his full stake on longer-priced horses, but I didn't pick as many of those at the time as I would in later years and it wasn't too much of a problem. Our association lasted about three years, and drew to a close only when my sudden move from Cambridge made it impossible to continue. Looking back at my figures he had no cause for complaint, as the bets I recommended to him showed a profit of 30 per cent. At the time there were still some big on-course layers and Michael, who received information from plenty of other sources as well, was able to ensure they were well accommodated.

I vividly recall some of the horses I recommended during those three years. I was particularly confident about the chances of Tregaron before he landed the White Rose Handicap at Ascot in May 1996. Word soon reached me that the biggest rails operator at the time, Stephen Little, had laid Michael a bet of £40,000 at 11-2, a wager that won him £220,000. Allowing for other outlets, his total winnings on the race must have been very impressive.

Three weeks later, I remember a trip to Bath to back For Old Times Sake in a two-year-old race. This time it was I who crossed swords at the track with Little. Little is a vicar's son and I'm told he was so keen on racing as a youngster that he cycled to every course in Britain. Later, of course, he travelled in much greater comfort as he made his name. My wager of £12,000 on For Old Times Sake at 15-8 was at the time my biggest individual bet with a single bookmaker, and I doubt if my agents have managed many bigger since. What amused me more than the result, which certainly put a smile on my face, was that I left straight after the race, the third on the card, only to see Little's enormous car – I think it was a Rolls – gliding out of the car park at the same time. Presumably he'd lost his appetite for any more business that day. Fair play to him – you'd struggle to find a course bookmaker to lay anyone a bet like that on a Saturday nowadays, never mind to a professional punter at a quiet midweek meeting at Bath.

Blue Goblin, in a six-furlong handicap at Newmarket in May

CHAPTER 3

NOT SUCH A MAGNIFICENT 7

THERE were better times, and many of them. There was one week in Ireland when we had enormous fun and collected plenty of money into the bargain, always a satisfying combination. At the time I had a hugely profitable account over there that laid large bets at morning prices. To avoid detection from the bookies' Veitch radar, I'd opened the account in the name of my assistant, Stuart Hudson.

Unfortunately, I'd spent weeks chasing payment, and had decided that if the mountain wouldn't come to Mohammed, then Mohammed would . . . well, you know what I mean. Two friends from university, David Craggs and Richard Lamb, joined me on a boys' week in Ireland, with the first two days encamped in the Dublin pub run by the bookmaker concerned. We drank his beer and got on his good side while waiting for him to pay up. During this time David and Richard had to remember to call me Stuart which, as the beer went down, became harder for them to do and also more hilarious.

After he paid up, we went on a trip round Ireland before meeting up with the bookie and his pals for a last night in Dublin. We were led astray in the bars and pubs and I became separated from David and Richard. Not only that, but at 4am I found myself being driven increasingly erratically round the dark and utterly unfamiliar suburbs of the city by the by-now-very-drunk bookie, with three of his equally hammered mates wedged into the back of the car. I got back to my hotel at about 7am, with barely enough time to have a much-needed dose of caffeine before heading off for the ferry.

The 1993 Derby was very profitable for me. That year, the racing world seemed obsessed with the unbeaten Tenby, the long-time ante-post favourite trained by Henry Cecil. However, he'd not impressed me in winning a five-runner Dante Stakes at York and I couldn't understand why he was set to start odds-on at Epsom. Cecil had another runner in Commander In Chief, a lightly raced colt with plenty of room for improvement, and I'd had a whisper that he was improving fast. His victory was very satisfying, as so many seemed convinced that Tenby was a good thing. It was well known in racing circles that I had backed and tipped Commander In Chief.

Wardara's victories in October 1994 created waves in a number of directions. She won a nursery at Newmarket for trainer Gay Kelleway and landed a bit of a tickle for some friends of mine who owned her. I wasn't involved that day, but the result produced a public storm of protest from tipster Ron Dawson, another owner in Kelleway's stable, who had been left out of the gamble and fell out with the trainer as a result.

Shortly before this furore, Dawson had ruined a gamble for another stable. I had been asked to place thousands of pounds on behalf of connections only to find that Dawson, an owner in that yard, had selected the horse as a maximum bet on his tipping service, something he had promised not to do. This torpedoed the gamble, yet Dawson was unrepentant, so the decision by Kelleway not to tell him about Wardara had been an astute one. Dawson was to get into serious trouble in later years over his handling of Classic Bloodstock and certainly didn't appear a popular figure in racing.

A follow-up win for Wardara at Newbury nine days later produced further controversy after I was asked to place some business for one of the owners. The winnings came to more than £10,000 and I had it posted in cash to the owner in Scotland. They say you should never send cash through the post – perhaps I should have taken the advice. A couple of months later, to my astonishment, a call came from an assistant of mine who had sent the registered envelopes. He was alarmed that Customs and Excise had arrived on his doorstep and were quizzing him in detail about the envelopes, as they suspected the owner of evading the betting tax in force at the time. Fortunately, we always kept meticulous records, and I was able to furnish my assistant with statements from the major bookmakers detailing every penny that had been placed. It was never going to be a problem, but it was a scary moment nonetheless for my assistant, who was just out of university and very shocked to find the authorities knocking on his door, suspecting him of illegal practice.

I was always scrupulously careful to ensure that I obeyed all the rules regarding betting tax and would not even agree to place a tax-free bet at the races for friends. Such activity was fairly common-place at the time. Nor would I agree to any side bets with friends for fear of being accused of not paying the betting duty. It was thus very frustrating when Betfair set up years later and I heard that they had discovered that legislation had not in fact been drafted to prevent parties betting with each other without tax, as long as no bookmaker was involved. This was annoying in the extreme, as I had spent years going out of my way to follow guidelines that turned out to be incorrect. Whoever drafted the original legislation for Customs and Excise should hang their heads in shame.

At around this time, a Scottish friend used to come down for Newmarket races with a group of pals, and this invariably led to a riotous couple of days. When they stayed with me they would arrive back at my house in dribs and drabs at all hours and mostly pass out downstairs. On one occasion they were receiving constant calls from a friend who bet heavily and successfully on football, and whose bets had all gone down when Cambridge United fielded a team of reserves. Their friend Tommy had phoned the Cambridge Clubcall number before the game and there had been no mention of reserves.

The next evening he was still livid and phoning his pals to complain as we were having dinner, breathing fire about the Cambridge manager who had failed to announce the changes. Thinking quickly, my friend said: "Well he's here the noo actually, do you wan' a wud with him?" He then passed me the phone. I must have done a convincing impression of an apologetic Cambridge manager because my bollocking from the world's most irate punter lasted fully 15 minutes.

Frankie Dettori's 'Magnificent 7' at Ascot in September 1996 was considerably less amusing, and unprofitable into the bargain. While virtually everyone applauded his extraordinary feat in winning every race on the card, I was left counting the cost of opposing him in the final race on Fujiyama Crest. As the odds about his chances in each of the later races tumbled, I was able to bet on the field against his mount, as bookmakers were keen to balance their books. Getting odds of 1-2 about Fujiyama Crest *not* winning the last race, when he had been 16-1 a couple of hours earlier, was too good to miss. Sadly, I didn't miss out.

I was not alone in thinking that Fujiyama Crest could not win under top weight in such a tough handicap. By the time of the last race the bookmakers were running for cover from a series of doubles, trebles, four-timers and accumulators on Dettori's mounts. As a result, a horse whose true odds should have been at least 16-1 was trading at 2-1. Any professional worthy of the name had to oppose Fujiyama Crest at those ridiculous odds, so by the time the race started I stood to win around £13,000 if any of his opponents won. Equally, I would lose £26,000 if he proved to be Dettori's final winner of the day.

I would not say that his fellow jockeys handed him the prize, but nor did they cover themselves with glory. Dettori's chance on Fujiyama Crest was certainly improved by the fact that not one jockey chose to take him on for the lead when he set such a slow pace. I absolve Pat Eddery of any blame here, as no-one could have tried harder than he on Northern Fleet to spoil the party in the finishing straight. Indeed, in the final 100 yards Fujiyama Crest was out on his feet, but somehow he hung on by a neck to complete a fairytale day for his jockey. With the inclusion of another losing bet, my losses of nearly £30,000 were a big hit. It was the most I'd lost in a day at that stage of my career – but it could have been worse. Several bookmakers took the same view as me, and some were put out of business when Fujiyama Crest scrambled over the line. Gary Wiltshire, for one, famously lost more than £1m by fielding against Fujiyama Crest. At least he survived to fight another day.

That June, I'd attempted a monster touch in the Wokingham Handicap at Royal Ascot with Green Perfume. He was drawn in stall two and there used to be some massive draw biases in the days before Ascot was redeveloped. It was an enormous advantage to be drawn under the stands' rail and, even better, there was a no-hoper alongside him in stall one. I'd backed Green Perfume at all rates down from 20-1 – he returned 13-2 favourite and I stood to win well into six figures and thus smash my previous biggest win. In addition, I'd made sure that the message had been passed through to the horse's connections that staying tight on the stands' rail would be an enormous advantage.

At halfway, Richard Quinn, who'd ridden the aforementioned Tregaron, was perfectly placed on the rail aboard Green Perfume, but he then seemed to panic and switched off the fence to manoeuvre past the leader. This took him off the magic carpet of faster ground and, in my view, easily cost him the length or so by which he was beaten. To add insult to financial injury, the eventual winner Emerging Market (drawn 7) came storming through on the rail where Green Perfume should have been. The BBC coverage made very little reference to the draw, as was often the case at the time, but I was certain that Quinn had blundered by switching off the rail.

The early days were a lot of fun, win or lose, but possibly the most fun day of all was when Clifton Fox won the 1996 November Handicap at Doncaster. Doubts had been expressed about Jeremy Glover's contender staying the trip of a mile and a half, seemingly because he'd won the Cambridgeshire over three furlongs shorter a month earlier. I wasn't worried that he was stepping up in distance, as I'd long thought that a mile and a half would suit him.

I backed Clifton Fox to win around £30,000 and advised Michael Tabor to have a thick bet as well. My friends at Pertemps, a recruitment company, had a box at Doncaster and on this occasion they entertained some local office staff who were being rewarded with a day at the races for achieving recent targets. Before the race, Pertemps chairman Tim Watts announced that he was placing £500 on Clifton Fox for the ten or so employees to split between them if he won. This produced a shocked silence, as the guests were mostly girls and I don't think any of them had bet more than a fiver before.

When Clifton Fox got up under Nigel Day to win a desperate finish by a neck there was uproar in the box, and I spent much of the next 20 minutes trying to celebrate while being hoisted off the floor by a group of revellers. We had managed to get the bet on at 10-1, and watching Tim count out £5,000 in cash for the overjoyed group was some sight. I've never seen winnings received by so many rapturous faces. I've only received two marriage proposals in my life, and both of them came in that 20-minute period.

CHAPTER 4

CALVIN HALL

I WAS in the bathroom getting ready for a night out when my door-bell rang. It was Thursday, June 25, 1998. Can you remember what you were doing on that date? I can. I wish I couldn't.

Five minutes earlier, I'd been thinking how well things were going. I was midway through a successful summer's betting and well on top of the heavy workload that involved. When the doorbell rang I assumed it was my ride into town, and called "Taxi?" out of the bathroom window. A stocky man I didn't recognise came into view and, in a tone loaded with aggression, said: "No."

I was still damp from the shower, but threw my clothes on and went downstairs. When I opened the door, there was a second man on the doorstep, a man I recognised as Calvin Hall. "You know me, Patrick, and this is my associate," Hall said. "We'd like to come in."

He meant that he was coming in. The use of the word 'associate', coming from two men on my doorstep, seemed chosen to mirror a famous scene in the film *Pulp Fiction*, a scene that was very bad news for those receiving the visit. The tone was menacing and, as both men were very heavily built, I wasn't in any position to argue.

I was immediately alarmed. Having already had the misfortune to be introduced to Hall, I had been warned that he had a terrible reputation locally. He exuded menace and was known to be the chief suspect in what was described as the gangland-style execution of a nightclub bouncer in Cambridge. Now he was standing in my hall-way, giving me a threatening look, next to an equally dangerous-looking accomplice. Both men looked bulked up by steroid use, both men were considerably larger than me. This was serious.

"You never returned my business plan and have cost me a lot of money," said Hall. "I didn't know you wanted it back," I replied, sounding a lot calmer than I felt. My heart was pounding. A few weeks earlier, an acquaintance had passed on an absurd five-page business plan, written in poor English. His accusation was ridiculous given that I hadn't been asked to return the plan, but it was obvious that this was merely an excuse to enable Hall to make demands.

"With what you have cost me, I need to be compensated," said Hall, ignoring my reply. He reached into his pocket and pulled out three plain white envelopes. "Pick one of these," he demanded.

"What is all this?" I replied. My pulse was still racing and now my palms were sweaty and my shirt felt hot and wet rather than damp. The fact that Hall seemed to be introducing a bizarre element of chance to the situation only served to create the impression that he might be unhinged as well as dangerous.

"Pick one of the envelopes," he snarled. I chose an envelope and was told to turn it over. '£70K' had been typed on the back. Heaven knows what had been typed on the other envelopes; I didn't want to think about it.

"That's the compensation you're going to pay me for costing me this deal," Hall said. "In the envelope are some bank account details. You are going to transfer that amount of money into that account tomorrow." His 'associate' then spoke for the first time: "Otherwise I'll come back tomorrow and break your legs." After a short pause, he added: "Or cut them off."

"I don't have that sort of money," I said. Now, I was petrified, but there was no chance of me handing over such a sum when I'd done nothing wrong. "You can get it," Hall's associate replied. Hall pushed his finger into my face and added: "You know what you've been told. It's to be done tomorrow." He reached over to grab the keys to my Mercedes from the shelf, adding: "I'm taking the car until the money's paid, just to make sure."

The two men turned and left, closing the door quietly behind them. The episode that would turn my life upside down had lasted less than five minutes. How had I become embroiled in this terrifying situation? Not through any fault of my own, that was for sure. Hall was clearly a highly dangerous figure and, despite the gambling industry having a colourful reputation, I'd never met anyone like him. I still lived on the university side of Cambridge, having stayed on after my three years there. The suburb of Newnham was leafy and peaceful, not in any way renowned for trouble. The first I'd heard of Hall was when an acquaintance, Jerome Davies, approached me at the gym one day. "An acquaintance of mine has a business proposition for you," he said. "I'll have his business plan sent round."

Davies and I shared a few friends and had sometimes been in the same group having a drink in the bar adjoining the gym, but I'd never really warmed to him. He was a talker, the sort of person who would frequently suggest that the next round was his although rarely actually buying one, so I'd given very little thought to what he had said. The business plan arrived a few days later. It was about five pages long, cheaply bound with a plastic clip. It contained supposed plans to open a complex of bars, restaurants, a nightclub and casino on a disused site in Cambridge. Such a scheme would have required a business plan of hundreds of pages. The proposal was badly written and ignored the reality that legislation at the time made it impossible to even apply for a casino licence in Cambridge.

The plan's marketing strategy was one poorly-written sentence long: "MARKETING: We will pay celebrities to visit our premises, hence making them more attractive to paying customers." I'd thrown the plan in the bin and thought nothing more of it.

A few days later, I received a call from a friend, Simon Hellowell, who sounded quite distressed. "Jerome Davies has been in touch with you, hasn't he?" he said. "He asked me for your number. Whatever you do, don't get involved. Calvin Hall is very, very bad news. Did you ever hear about a nightclub bouncer called Adam Fraser who was shot dead? There's talk that Hall did it." He repeated: "Whatever you do, don't get involved."

"Don't worry," I replied. "The plan didn't make any sense, so there's no way I'd do business with him anyway." Simon seemed reassured and I hoped that was the end of the matter. A couple of weeks later, Davies telephoned me. "There's a bit of a problem," he said. "My friend, the one who sent you the business plan, didn't get it back. He's upset about it and he's talking of sending some boys to see you."

"What are you talking about?" I replied. "He never asked for it back. Anyway, it was five pages of nonsense. It didn't have a hope in hell of getting off the ground." Davies didn't appear to be listening. "Nah, well, he wanted it back and apparently he's sending some boys round to come and see you."

"I still don't understand what you are talking about," I replied. After repeating himself a couple more times, Davies added: "I think I can get him to come round and see you so that you can straighten this out. That way there'll be no need for his men to visit." The story seemed very bizarre. I was increasingly concerned after Simon's earlier warning. "Well, if he really has to," I told Davies. "I don't see why there was any need to involve me in this in the first place."

Hall arrived at my house half an hour later. Even in smart clothing it was clear that he was physically very strong. He also had an intimidating air and stared at me throughout our conversation. Otherwise, he was calm and polite. He suggested that I should think again about his business plan, and an investment of £100,000 was mentioned. Not wanting to upset him, I claimed not to have any spare funds.

He asked if I could find someone else to invest. Hoping he would leave, I said I would do my best. The discussion lasted another few minutes, but it was still very unsettling having a man with such a bad reputation sitting in my living room. Hall then insisted that I drive away with him and follow his car to a disused building about a mile across Cambridge. This was the site around which his 'business plan' was based. During a brief chat there he explained excitedly how successful his plans were going to be. Having seen the business plan, I knew that he was living in a dream world. The conversation seemed ludicrous, so I just aimed to placate him and was pleased to get away, having reiterated that I would attempt to find an investor.

Hall had phoned me a few days later, a conversation in which I said that I was still looking for an investor but hadn't had any luck yet. That was the last I heard until Hall and his 'associate' turned up on my doorstep a couple of weeks later.

Returning to my immediate predicament, the first question in my mind was why had Davies introduced me to someone who was such bad news? I had no answer. I heard rumours later that Davies had lent money to Hall and had subsequently been told that he needed to find an investor if he wanted the money repaid.

Presumably Davies simply chose someone that he knew was quite wealthy. I was well known at the gym as a successful gambler, and if I didn't arrive in the Mercedes that Hall drove away in, then I'd pull up in a Ferrari. It was obvious even at a half-glance that I had plenty of disposable income. Clearly Hall had decided that I was a suitable candidate to be his unwilling investor. He had evidently been hoping that I might invest in his absurd scheme purely out of fear. I've since heard that he had persuaded people to do just that, coercing them into handing over maybe £5,000, or £2,000, because they were too frightened to turn him down. Hall had clearly decided to seek a much bigger sum from me and, following my refusal, he was now simply demanding money with menaces.

I was now faced with the biggest quandary of my life. My heart was still pounding, although its pace had slowed. My shirt was damp with a cold sweat, a strange feeling on a warm night in June. But I had to try to clear my head and decide what to do. I'd done nothing wrong, and on principle wasn't paying Hall 70p, never mind £70,000. I could have stood my ground, refused to pay and stayed in Cambridge, but that would have meant living in fear, forever waiting for a knock on the door in the middle of the night.

I wasn't prepared to give Hall the chance to come back and make good on his threats, so I'd have to go to the police. But that meant I was putting my life on the line. Word had it that the last person to get seriously on the wrong side of Hall had ended up dead. After Hall's first visit to my house, I'd found out more about the murder of Adam Fraser. It wasn't a murder committed in the heat of the moment after an argument had got out of hand. Fraser had been lured to waste ground and shot dead at point-blank range in a gangland execution. It had been a planned and cold-blooded killing.

Hall would eventually be charged with the murder. When the case came to court, evidence would be heard that Hall had told a third party that "Fraser took two in the head". The trial would end in a hung jury, meaning that some but not all of the jury were convinced beyond reasonable doubt of Hall's guilt. The CPS were insistent on bringing the case again, but this time it fell through. It would be years later before Hall would finally be given a long-term sentence for attempted murder after a psychopathic and near-fatal stabbing of a police officer.

However, at the moment Hall was very much still at large. No-one had dared to testify against him in a major case, and although I was scared witless at the prospect of doing so I knew that it had to be done. I also knew that if I did so, I risked becoming the next person to die from 'two in the head'. I would have to be incredibly careful.

My only advantage was that I could choose to disappear completely. I had a good life in Cambridge but, with no family or long-term roots in the area, a rapid move elsewhere was possible. My only option was to make sure that neither Hall nor anyone connected to him could find me. There were problems implicit in this, as although I could recognise Hall, I was far from confident of identifying his partner, even if the police could find him. I've never been good at remembering faces and, in the brief time the two men had spent at my house, my eyes had nearly always been on Hall. And even if both men were caught, I'd still have no guarantees as to who else might come looking for me.

The decision to go to the police meant bringing an end to life as I knew it. In the months to come, I'd go to whatever lengths were necessary to ensure my safety. I'd remove myself completely from friends and family. I would live a very secluded life, mentally and physically withdrawn from the people I knew and cared about. I was mentally strong, but at the outset didn't know how much this way of existence would take its toll. I would find myself changing completely into a much more withdrawn mental state, one that would take years to fully recover from. To this day, the emotions connected to these events are the ones that define me. They come back to me many times each month. If I have a sad or difficult moment, they'll come back to me and push me on. Even in the happiest moments, when I had my first winner as an owner at Royal Ascot, my thoughts will go back to what I had to go through to get there. At a moment of triumph, those around me will often notice a moment or two when I am strangely subdued.

Leaving the city that had become my home would be very sad. I had worked so hard on my business from the moment I arrived in

Cambridge and now, within a few tense minutes of Hall's departure, I knew I would never spend another night in my own house. The taxi I had booked earlier now arrived, and I decided I might as well still take it. I was due to meet a friend and badly needed to talk to someone before going to the police. Harvey Cyzer, son of now-retired trainer Charles and later a trainer himself, was assistant to the legendary Henry Cecil at the time. He was stunned when I told him what had happened, and agreed that if I was going to involve the police I should do it as soon as possible.

He drove me back to my house. Concerned that Hall might reappear at any moment, I quickly packed a suitcase. I was in the house for less than ten minutes. Harvey said that I could stay with him in Newmarket after I left the police station, which was a brave offer considering the people we were dealing with. I thanked him, and he drove away, leaving me alone and facing a trip to the police station.

I decided to take the Ferrari with me. In doing so, what I lost in subtlety and secrecy I gained in the guarantee that I'd have enough speed to shake off anyone who pursued me. I drove to Parkside police station in Cambridge, taking a circuitous route to make sure I wasn't being followed. How quickly my life had changed. Once there, I gave only the barest details to the duty officer, who explained that as it was just after 9pm, he doubted whether anybody from CID would appear until the next shift started at 10pm. He then showed me into a tiny interview room and left me alone.

The room had three chairs and a small table. With its poor lighting and cheap paint flaking off the walls, it felt almost like a cell. I felt very alone, and had an overwhelming urge to speak to someone. It seemed wise to involve as few people as possible – in their interests and mine – but I decided to telephone my gardener Jonathan. He also worked on his family's market stall in the centre of town and was the most streetwise person I knew in Cambridge. I called him and asked if he could find out more about Calvin Hall. He rang back a few minutes later, sounding agitated, and said he'd been told that all the rumours were true, or worse, and that he wanted to stay well clear of the situation.

I put the phone on the table and stared at the wall. Five minutes later, Jonathan called again, emotion clear in his voice. Despite what he had been told, he'd decided to come to the police station to prevent me from going through such an ordeal alone. This was a courageous move from someone who was very easily connected to me by Cambridge people and I remembered it years later when the time came to do him a favour. He stayed at the police station for the rest of the evening, which was to last another six and a half hours.

Shortly after 10pm, a woman in her mid-twenties walked into the room and introduced herself as the detective on duty. She was holding a slip of paper which, among other things, included what seemed to be a one-line summary of my predicament supplied by the reception officer. £70K OR HIS LEGS. Not much beating around the bush there, then. I was amazed at how succinctly my troubles had been summed up. Four words had changed my life. It seemed very matter of fact.

I didn't name Hall initially, as I was keen to see what assurances I would receive about my security when the case came to court. The arrival of a detective chief inspector shortly after midnight, wearing hastily donned gardening jeans, made it clear that the police were taking matters very seriously. After I received suitable assurances, I named Hall at 2am, but it would take another two hours before the 14-page statement was written up. Discussions with the DCI confirmed that Hall was considered the most dangerous man in the area and that they had wanted to see him taken off the streets for years. The police were keen to take me into their own protection, but this didn't fit in with my plans. I didn't want anyone else to know where

I was unless it was absolutely necessary. I would do this my way.

I left the police station at 4am. Back in my car, the eerily quiet feel of that hour was magnified by my situation. Darkest just before the dawn? I can attest to that. The journey out of Cambridge would become a painfully familiar routine, as from that day on I rarely drove anywhere directly. I left Cambridge in the wrong direction, then drove around for long enough to make certain I wasn't being followed. Finally, I cut across a country road to join the correct route some miles away from the city. Despite the obvious speed advantage of my Ferrari, I knew it wasn't the right car to be driving and that I would soon need to find a more discreet method of travel.

The next day was starting as the worst day of my life was ending. I didn't relax for a moment, eyes peeled for anything out of the ordinary. Every time an object on the roadside was lit up by my headlights, my eyes darted around looking for trouble. There were no dangers in this peaceful country morning, but I was in no fit state to make rational judgments. Harvey let me in to his home in Newmarket at around 4.45am and I went straight to bed.

CHAPTER 5

SWAP WITH ANYONE?

IT TAKES a couple of seconds after waking to recall where life was left off the night before. So, when I woke, I had the extremely dubious pleasure of renewing acquaintance with the memory of the night before, and I realised again that my life as I knew it had ended. It was around 9am. I was alone in the house, as Harvey and his girlfriend had left for work. All I had on me were the keys to the Ferrari.

I looked at them and told myself I had two choices: either get in the car and drive it straight into a wall at top speed, or accept my predicament and start life all over again. I stared out of the window for a moment or two and then, picking up the keys, I walked out to the car. A minute later, I was back in the house with my suitcase. This would have to be day one of my new life. A long struggle lay ahead.

How was I to go about disappearing completely? I had some savings, had the necessary determination, but knew that almost anybody can be found given sufficient time and resources. I knew nothing about security, so expert advice was required. The first job was to make contact with the police, and an arrangement was made to meet that afternoon. They wanted me to travel to Parkside but I refused, wary of the possibility that someone could be watching, so I would check into a room at the Post House hotel on the outskirts of Cambridge, thus avoiding the need to drive into the city. The police would meet me there.

Their plan involved my contacting Calvin Hall so that they could record our telephone conversations for evidence. The police had originally been keen for me to meet Hall while wearing a wiretap, but I was only prepared to do so with the guarantee of armed protection. I talked to detective superintendent Negus, who said that it was not police policy to carry live guns in a public place unless absolutely necessary, so to my relief this idea fell through. I was sick to my stomach at the prospect of having to meet Hall again.

It was now a matter of urgency for me to find a more discreet vehicle. Throwing on a baseball cap and sunglasses, the only disguise I had available, I walked into Newmarket, keeping to the quiet back streets. It was the first time I'd been anywhere on foot since Hall's visit. As with the journey from Cambridge, my eyes darted in all directions behind the sunglasses. Walking around unprotected had my heart pounding again.

On the way, I telephoned a racing friend who also dealt in second-hand cars. By the time I reached the taxi rank, I'd established that a car auction was in the vicinity and arranged a meeting there. Three hours later, I was the not-so-proud owner of a five-year-old Renault, one of the more basic models. As there was no room for frills, Mercedes or Ferraris in my plan, I chose the most inconspicuous car I could find. My racing contact had travelled a long way to meet me at the auction. He was curious about my plans, and kept repeating the wisecrack that 'a friend in need is a f***king nuisance'. It was, as I'm sure you can imagine, a great help.

The journey back from the auction was spent on the mobile. The directory service gave me numbers for various private detective agencies, and I phoned them posing as a potential client who needed to find someone. How my life had changed, and how swiftly. Twenty-four hours earlier I was studying the videos from Royal Ascot the previous week. Now I was engaged in the bizarre process of extracting information from private detectives.

Piece by piece, I extracted hints about how missing people were tracked down. These ranged from obvious sources, like the electoral roll and information held about directors at Companies House, to all sorts of other techniques. I was told about the trails that people leave in life, such as via their credit cards or when their car passes through cameras that record the licence plate. Even a mobile is sending a constant signal of the owner's whereabouts. Much of this information should not really be available to the public, but there were one or two hints that it could be accessed if needed.

I knew I needed ongoing expert advice. One agency seemed particularly professional and I hinted that I was actually on the other side, someone who needed to vanish completely. They recommended a security consultant and passed on some details. It was a condition of the arrangement that I didn't reveal his name, so I shall refer to him from now on as Michael Thornton. Michael's advice did not come cheap. Over the course of many months I would pay him a substantial five-figure sum that included invoices for occasions when I needed security personnel to watch over me.

It was not in my nature to leave any stone unturned in guaranteeing my safety. Betting professionally had taught me to be thorough and my new situation only enhanced this. I would take a very clinical approach to removing any possible risk. Paying substantial costs and dealing with security procedures was the only way to minimise the danger. All the time, I was very aware that it was believed that Hall's last victim had died from a bullet in the head.

Back in Newmarket, I bought a pay-as-you-go mobile and made sure that I had a secure place to stow it where it would not be found. This phone was used only to call Michael and only when I was on my own. At around 3pm it was time to head back to Cambridge to meet the police. I had my face well covered and was driving my new low-profile car, but was still extremely fearful of returning. I kept thinking about the Fraser murder and the type of person I was dealing with.

What sort of man goes to the house of someone he has met only once, involves him in a bizarre ritual of selecting an envelope, and then threatens to carry out grievous bodily harm?

I had insisted that the police place a protection team at our chosen hotel, just in case Hall, or someone close to him, happened to be there. I wasn't willing to take any chances. The police had assured me that I wouldn't recognise their plain-clothes security, but I rather suspected that the man walking the car park with an Alsatian and the man with a hand-held radio near reception may have been involved. Still, I wanted to be safe, so I was just pleased they were there.

I was joined in the hotel room by the chief inspector, detective sergeant Barr and a police communications expert who would attach a device to my mobile to record any calls. They briefed me on what to say when Hall called, underlining that it was vital to mention that I was scared by what had happened the night before. I was confident of fulfilling that part of the brief. Even if Hall didn't repeat any of his threats, the recording would still hamper his chances of inventing a plausible defence.

Hall used a pager for contact, which at the time was apparently common among criminals who knew that their movements could be traced if they carried a mobile. After the briefing, I phoned a pager message through to Hall. He called back quickly, evidently keen to hear how his demand for £70,000 was progressing. I told him that obtaining the funds was proving difficult and that I was too scared to meet him. He was extremely guarded on the phone and kept repeating that I had to meet him, and suggested that "phones were bad things". Just speaking to Hall was immensely nerve-wracking but I managed to stay fairly calm.

The call ended with the agreement that I would continue my endeavours to secure the funds and contact Hall after the weekend. The police were clearly encouraged by this initial contact. Although Hall was distinctly cautious, the fact that he had not replied with "what on earth are you talking about?" would make it very hard to invent a defence in court. I arranged to phone the police again on

Monday and left the hotel. The man with the Alsatian was still patrolling the car park.

I had planned to travel with friends to the Irish Derby that weekend, and at the moment spending a few days in another country was extremely tempting. Although I would be in a public place, nobody from Cambridge knew of my trip and the crowd at the Curragh would be enormous. Michael was in agreement, with the proviso that I didn't discuss any of my future plans with my party of friends.

I had improved my disguise by the time I arrived at Stansted airport on the Saturday. Michael told me that false beards and moustaches, invariably used by undercover characters in films, were rarely used in real life. Changing someone's appearance properly on a film set took up to four hours a day. The sensible approach would always be to conceal rather than change, and hats, dark glasses and high collars were the key elements. I'd look a little over-dressed for the summer, but passers-by would probably assume I had a bad cold. To be fair, I wasn't really bothered what the general public assumed.

If they were anything like the six or seven friends I was travelling with, Joe Public would be having a good laugh about it, because when I met them in a bar at the airport they'd already had a few and greeted the covered-up undercover Veitch with considerable hilarity. I didn't think it was very funny at all – what was happening to me was no laughing matter – and then felt rather guilty for dampening their holiday mood with a brief, terse explanation.

The weekend passed without incident apart from long periods of brooding. I was deep in thought the whole time, never able to relax. I wanted my old life in Cambridge back, but had to face the reality that it wasn't going to happen. On Monday morning, at Dublin airport for the return flight, I became paranoid that someone would be waiting for me at Stansted. As the only people who knew I was in Ireland were with me, this was clearly illogical, but such was my mental state that logic wasn't an option. An overpowering sense of danger hit me. I devised a solution with the support of a couple of friends – at Stansted, I would stay in the baggage area until they located the police on duty. It was all just a question of reassurance, really, but thankfully two policemen obliged in escorting me back to the car. I drove back to Harvey's house and spent the rest of the day indoors.

The police wanted to meet me on Tuesday to record another call with Hall. A new venue was needed because the recording quality from the hotel phone call was poor. They wanted me to take a call on my mobile at the police station, where the recording equipment would work better. They managed to overcome my wariness by convincing me that I was highly unlikely to be spotted with my face well covered, and that Hall could hardly be expected to be mounting a 24-hour watch on all the local police stations, five days after he threatened me.

I left early for Parkside, as the journey to Cambridge was its now-customary three times the normal duration. Newmarket is east of Cambridge, so I arrived from the west. With the benefit of hindsight, these precautions might seem excessive, but at the time the overwhelming need was to minimise every possible risk and this was just one part of that process.

In the CID unit, I recorded another conversation with Hall, once again playing for time. This wasn't as excruciating the second time around, as speaking from the police station was more reassuring than working up a cold sweat in an unknown hotel room, and I'd been assured that the police planned to arrest Hall within days. Having spent every hour of five days worrying about him, this was therapeutic to say the least. Before leaving, I collected a police grade panic alarm. You can buy panic alarms in shops, but not one like this, as when the key was pulled out it emitted a piercing siren that would have stopped a ship in full sail. From that day on, I would get into the habit of carrying one.

On the way back to Newmarket, Harvey called. His father, who owned the house and had never even met me, was understandably concerned when he found out that a fugitive from a suspected murderer was in hiding at his property. I could see his point of view. I was grateful for the time I'd been able to spend there, and had planned to leave the area completely in a few days anyway, but it was time to move now. My suitcase was already outside in the garage when I got back.

I had to find somewhere with no connection to my old life, so chose Bury St Edmunds, about 45 minutes' drive away, for a very temporary bolthole. I'd never been there before. My Ferrari, which had been locked in Harvey's garage, needed to be put into storage, so I took it to a friend, Paul Walters, who had an unused garage in a quiet location. On Michael's advice, I checked into a low-grade hotel in Bury St Edmunds under an assumed name. He had told me to avoid the nicer hotels, as they would be a more obvious starting point for anyone looking for me.

Despair washed over me as I walked into my room. There were a few people who knew what had happened to me, but it was essential that I distance myself from them completely. In protecting my life, I was cutting myself off from those closest to me. That evening, it seemed as though the whole country was watching England's World Cup match against Argentina in France, the game in which David Beckham was sent off for kicking an opponent. I knew lots of friends would have got together to watch the game on TV, but here I was frightened to death, alone in a dingy hotel room with a packet of biscuits for my dinner.

Before all this happened, when the good times were at their best, I'd sometimes use the expression 'I wouldn't swap with anyone'.

Looking round the bleak room and reviewing my situation, I said out loud: "Swap with anyone."

Next morning, it was time to leave the area completely. Michael had told me that the house of a discreet friend was far safer than a hotel. If I remained in the same hotel I would invite curiosity as to why I was staying there for so long. Renting a flat in an assumed name would not be easy, as the landlord and utility companies would require proof of identity. He also advised that London was much the best place to remain anonymous.

So I called David Craggs, a good friend from university, and he didn't hesitate to offer his help. I could install myself in David's spare room in a quiet corner of Wimbledon. On the journey down, it was time to permanently switch off my old mobile. I was aware that it was creating a trace of my movements and that Hall had the number, and as I was heading for London I wanted the last traceable point to be a long way from my new life. I drove 30 miles north of Cambridge before switching it off.

CHAPTER 6

I'LL NEED THE SHOTGUN PLATE

A S IT happened, I had to make an unexpected return to Cambridge the very next day. I picked up a message from the police, who were almost ready to arrest Hall but still did not have quite the quality of recording they needed. They needed Hall to ring my landline number, which meant returning to my house. This would at least allow me time to pack up some more belongings under the umbrella of police protection, and might make Hall think that I was still in Cambridge, which would help in trying to conceal my true movements. I remember thinking how important an issue removing Hall from the streets had become, based on the number of police man-hours devoted to ensuring that my evidence was irrefutable.

As I didn't want to be seen returning to my house, I met DS Barr a few miles away, lay down in the back of his unmarked car, and stayed there until it was safely out of sight in my garage with the door shut. Once again, this may seem extreme, but I just wasn't prepared to take any chances, knowing that the chief suspect in a murder might have guessed that I'd gone to the police and already had me down as his next victim.

My brief conversation with Hall proved difficult, much harder than the previous call. He had become even more guarded and seemed highly suspicious during our short exchange. This strategy had run its course, although thankfully the police felt they had enough evidence to make an arrest. I returned to London feeling drained. I hadn't expected to be needed again by the police and Hall's suspicion on the phone was very unsettling.

The following day brought another call from the police, this time welcome news. Their front-line team had broken down Hall's front door at dawn that morning. He wasn't there, so the police paged him, and within two hours he arrived at Parkside, by all accounts looking calm and confident. I had wondered whether there was any chance that the police would fail to press charges, on the basis that it was my word against his, but I kept recalling the expression on the DCI's face that first night when I named Calvin Hall. Having finally found somebody to testify, he'd had the look of someone who was determined to put his man behind bars. Hall was arrested as soon as he arrived at the police station, and I was told that they played him the tapes of our conversations at the subsequent interview.

That wasn't all the good news either – my Mercedes had turned up. In an act of shocking boldness, Hall had driven to the police station in my car, which he parked around 100 yards away down a side street with the key hidden in the exhaust. It would be some time before it was returned to me, as it was required for fingerprinting and other tests because there were suspicions that it had been used for other criminal purposes after it was stolen from me.

With Hall under arrest, I was left to adapt to a life in hiding. I had no choice but to wait for the court case, which the police hoped would be brought before the end of the year. My biggest problem was the lack of anything to keep me busy. David worked very long hours in the City and was often away at weekends, so I was almost always alone in his flat. My routine, such as it was, involved day after day of mind-numbing boredom, much of it spent watching TV or just sitting around feeling sorry for myself. I still had reason to be very concerned, because Hall's accomplice was still at large and would now know that I had called the police and assisted them in recording evidence. For all he knew I might have a perfect recollection of his face and be ready to identify him, as well as testifying against Hall.

When I ventured into public, it was hard to relax and I found myself spending every second scanning my surroundings for signs of anything untoward. It was no way to live. A balance had to be struck between remaining safe and seeking out enough human contact to keep my sanity, otherwise I would go downhill fast. Michael was able to arrange background security on occasions when I wanted to spend longer in public places, and after further discussions we decided that I could meet one or two friends occasionally, provided that this did not involve revealing my new location. As the weeks went by, I told a few more people what had happened.

I could travel to meet friends well away from London and Cambridge, but would park around half a mile from the meeting point, completing the journey on foot so that my new vehicle would remain a secret. This development, liberating though it seemed on one hand, provided only brief respite from the banality of my existence and the journey home would find me in despair once more, thinking only of the monotony that faced me on my return. It was also possible, very occasionally, to meet friends who lived in London. I would say that I was in town for a day or two the following weekend and organise a night out, at the end of the night remembering to be careful to leave in the direction of the hotel I had claimed to be using.

Avoiding my location being discovered was top priority. One friend might talk to another who might then talk to an acquaintance, with the result that my whereabouts would in turn become widely known. Even if friends managed to remain discreet there was always the danger that they might receive a visit from someone looking for me. Everything I did was accomplished with secrecy in mind. I didn't use my credit cards when in London to avoid creating a trail. I also had to leave town if I needed a doctor or dentist, registering as a holiday patient in an unrelated location. These were the details that might be checked by someone very keen to find me.

I couldn't expect to impose on David forever, so the next step would involve renting a flat in central London. I hoped this would ultimately prove to be a base for me to work the following year, as my share investments were going through a rough patch and I would need to be earning again by the time the next Flat season came around. On one of my 'visits' to London I had a night out with two friends and discovered that they were planning to rent a flat together. I decided to take them into my confidence and offer myself up as a third flatmate. The biggest advantage of sharing a flat was that nothing needed to be in my name. I was lucky to have two reliable friends who understood the gravity of my situation and wouldn't gossip about their hidden co-tenant.

I needed a semi-permanent assumed name for a few familiar situations, such as joining a gym. Michael suggested that I keep Patrick as my first name, as people in my position apparently found it very difficult to adapt to that degree of change, frequently failing to respond when addressed by their new first name and blowing their cover. Patrick stayed, then, and I chose a new surname for my time in London. One of my new flatmates lent me one of his credit cards to assist with situations where a card was required, such as checking into a hotel. Using someone else's credit card was against the law, but if I was caught out I felt confident that I was sufficiently valuable to the police for a prosecution to be unlikely.

My life – or rather, my existence – continued in this unsettled, unsettling fashion through the summer. In September, however, I received news that shook me to the core. It was one of those moments in your life when you can remember exactly where you were at the time. I picked up a voicemail informing me that Calvin Hall, who was on remand for his offences against me, had also been charged over the murder of Adam Fraser.

I should have been prepared for this – it was after all common knowledge that he was the chief suspect – but the news that he had been charged seemed to emphasise how dangerous Hall was. Apparently witnesses who were previously too scared to speak out were finally willing to testify against him now that he was behind bars.

In October, I was told that my presence was required in court for the case against Hall the following month. I immediately sought assurances that I would have the necessary police protection, as a security team supplied by Michael would not have the appropriate access in court, but when I spoke to DS Negus he said that security was not available owing to budget problems. Given that Hall's accomplice was still at large, I made my displeasure clear, but seemed to be coming up against a brick wall. A decision had already been taken. I knew the police badly needed me to be in court, and played the last card I had at my disposal, saying: "I have to tell you that I will do my best to turn up, but if something untoward happens between now and then, you must understand that I will not be there."

Negus countered: "Patrick, we are keen to stay on good terms with you and I appreciate that you've allowed us to go this far, but we will insist you come to court and if necessary we will issue a warrant for your arrest to ensure you do so." Months of subterfuge and misery had hardened my resolve. This wasn't how it was going to be. I wasn't going to back down.

I stayed calm, and replied in as matter-of-fact a tone as I could muster. "If I think that my life is in danger, then not only will I not appear in court but I'll also cease to exist. There will be no Patrick Veitch and you'll never hear from or see me again." I meant it, and I sensed that he knew it. Although my funds were dwindling, I still had the resources to leave the country and start afresh if needed. We left it at that. Two days later I received a message confirming that two police protection officers had been assigned.

Michael had decided against my wearing a bulletproof jacket day to day, as the risk of making me look more conspicuous outweighed the benefits, but he advised that one was needed for court. There was a choice: a jacket with protection against a handgun, or a jacket with an additional thick metal plate to withstand the use of a shotgun. This immediately provided a chilling reminder of a story the police had told me about Hall in the weeks before his arrest. Embroiled in an argument at Mitcham's Corner, a very public area in Cambridge, he had reached into the boot of his car, calmly pulled out a shotgun and pointed it at the other party. No shots were fired, but it was enough to make the question a straightforward one to answer. "I'll need the shotgun plate," I said.

The day before the trial, Michael warned me: "Don't look Hall in the eye during your testimony. You have nothing to gain by doing so. You are just a victim of crime, there to do your job in court and then be on your way. Don't make it any more personal that it needs to be."

This came as a nasty shock. How much more personal could it be? I'd lost so much of the life I knew and my financial assets were dwindling rapidly, but through it all I'd been fortified by the knowledge that I'd get to look Calvin Hall in the eye in court when the time finally came. I reminded Michael that I'd given up 99 per cent of my life, and the forthcoming confrontation with Hall in the dock was what I'd been waiting for.

"There you are, you've just said it," said Michael. "I don't understand," I said. "I am not in the business of making you satisfied. I'm in the business of keeping you safe," he replied, before explaining: "You say you've given up 99 per cent of your life, so you've already proved you can make sacrifices. Tomorrow you are going to make one more sacrifice by giving up your plan of looking him in the eye."

Early on the first day of the trial, I met the police protection team. I was installed in the court waiting room in plenty of time, along with the two police officers and a copy of my statement. They didn't know anything about my case and asked if they could read the statement. There was a noticeable change in their demeanour after they had read it. It was as if they seemed more determined to guarantee my safety now that they knew what had happened to me. Shortly afterwards, there was a knock on the door, and I heard a court officer explain that Jerome Davies had arrived as a witness and needed to join us in the waiting room.

I had not seen Davies since leaving Cambridge and hadn't planned on ever doing so, either. Having brought Hall into my life, he was the cause of all my troubles. Although I'm not a believer, in my mind I had the strong impression that I'd see him next when I called in to hell to watch him burning for what he'd done to me.

My protection officers must have seen that my expression had changed in an instant from composed to shocked. I could feel the blood draining away from my face. I didn't know the full background of Davies's connection to Hall and was horrified at the prospect of being in the same room as him. One of the protection officers told the court officer: "He's not coming in." The court officer insisted that Davies was to wait in there, but he was told again: "He's not coming in." I'd found two new friends here.

Events proceeded smoothly once my turn came to testify. On the way into court I'd had time for a quick handshake with DS George Barr, my closest police contact since June. We didn't speak but nodded, as if to indicate that there would be no mistakes from here. I gave my evidence to the prosecution barrister and negotiated a few simple attempts by the defence counsel to trip me up. He had a habit of asking questions that assumed something that was incorrect and contradicted my previous evidence, so I had to be careful to correct

63

the question rather than answer it. This left him with no choice but to suggest that I'd come to court to lie, and as I was a gambler by profession I wasn't really to be trusted. I replied that I might be a gambler but I was rather a good one and it didn't affect my ability to tell the truth. An appreciative chuckle ran around the courtroom.

During the break for lunch, I was told that the judge had asked the court clerk about the two very large gentlemen sitting in the witness gallery. He was evidently concerned they were connected to Hall, and apparently used the words "Who are those two heavies over there?" The judge was referring to my protection officers and was quickly reassured.

As I finished giving evidence, I noticed a juror with his arms folded staring at Hall with an angry expression on his face. By then I wasn't really in any doubt about the verdict, but it was comforting to get such a clear hint in my favour when I was still in the witness box. I left court and Cambridge that afternoon, with the second day of the trial due to continue without me. Michael had suggested that there was no benefit in my staying in court once my role was over. I would get the result by telephone soon enough. As expected, late on the second day I received word that Hall had been convicted. Apparently the jury was out for 25 minutes, barely time for them to travel in and out of court, elect a foreman and complete the formalities.

The judge was clearly just as horrified at the evidence as the juror I'd spotted, and said that he found it chilling that I'd been forced to leave Cambridge permanently and go into hiding. He then sentenced Hall to five years in prison. I'd hoped for longer.

As I bade farewell to my police protection team, one of them gave me his telephone number and suggested I gave him a call if I ever felt the need. Although they had been very supportive, Michael's advice was to avoid having any unnecessary ties with Cambridge, and that was the end of my life there except for one postscript.

I didn't tell my parents about my ordeal for many months, as I felt it was not safe for them to know too much. Instead, I told them that I was spending most of my time on an extended summer holiday on the south coast, thus avoiding a number of suggested meetings when my parents happened to be passing through Cambridge. However, eventually the excuses ran out, and I had to meet them for dinner at a quiet restaurant five miles outside the city. I spent that night in a bleak roadside motel a further five miles away. It was cold and dark and miserable, an eerie end to my time in Cambridge.

Back in London, I still needed to be very careful. Hall may have been behind bars, but his 'associate' could be stalking me, preparing to carry out a revenge attack for testifying against Hall. The fate of John and Joan Stirland, in 2004, was later to show the dangers that can still exist even after relocating. The couple had fled the Nottingham area after their son had angered local gangsters. They moved to a seaside bungalow in Lincolnshire, but word had reached Nottingham of their whereabouts. Mrs Stirland phoned the local police one night to report a prowler. The next day they were found murdered.

Michael told me that the public's perception of what it means to be in real danger tends to be very different from reality. The public are more used to danger as it is portrayed in films. In a movie, for dramatic effect, someone in peril will become aware of a whole series of warnings as the danger closes in. Michael said that people in real-life danger don't get those warnings. If the wrong person found them, they could change from alive to dead in the blink of an eye. We knew I was in real-life danger. The last person to get seriously on the wrong side of Hall had taken 'two in the head'.

At times, I felt like a fugitive in hiding. For a start, I wasn't going to meet many girls while locked away most of the time in my flat. When I did eventually meet someone, a producer for BBC radio, it led to another security problem. I gave away very few details about myself to her and was having fun, but there was a complication. She had fallen out with an ex-boyfriend who was then charged with assaulting her. What I hadn't known was that the ex-boyfriend read the news on Radio 1.

It must have been a quiet day for news, because when I turned up to watch the trial from the public gallery there were photographers everywhere. I managed to stay out of any pictures, but the next day I was amazed to find that most of the tabloids had the story on the front page, with headlines like 'I've been Newsbeaten'. Although the court case quickly collapsed, I remained uneasy about the publicity, and shortly afterwards we went our separate ways.

In late 1998, my life appeared to have come to a complete standstill. Hall's trial was over, but it was still much too soon to feel safe. I was waiting impatiently for his murder trial. If he was convicted, then he would be completely out of the picture and no doubt his followers would find better things to do with their time. I also clung to the belief that once a host of prosecution witnesses had testified against him in a murder trial, it would make anyone close to him lose interest in me.

It made sense to stay hidden away but there was very little for me to do. From a work point of view, I needed the turf Flat season to begin, and that was far away in late March. It proved an almost unbearable period for me, as gradually I sank into a deep depression and did less and less each day. Every morning, I dragged myself out of bed as far as the couch to watch TV, videos or DVDs. I watched endless episodes of Friends, and when nothing better was on I would sit in front of *The Full Monty*. I liked the film, but the Steve Harley track 'Come Up and See Me' upset me. No-one ever came up to see me. Only my two flatmates knew where I lived. That was the procedure. I remember the first time that a friend called round to see me unannounced. It was in 2002, four years after Calvin Hall's threats had forced me into hiding. It's the type of thing you don't miss until it never happens.

I was in a serious rut. Week after week went past and all the time the only thing happening was that I was getting poorer. I was earning nothing and my flat was expensive, as were the costs of ensuring my safety. I ran out of my original cash reserves in January and had to take out a loan against my Ferrari. Two months later, I managed to complete the sale of my house in Cambridge without ever meeting the estate agent, which raised some much-needed funds once I'd paid off the mortgage. When the remainder of the money arrived, most of it was already committed. Much more of this and my finances would be in dire trouble. A nine-month break in earnings combined with a huge increase in expenses was something I hadn't budgeted for.

I'm sure many will scoff at the idea of a hard-up Ferrari owner, but I was weeks away from having to sell everything I possessed, including my cars. In the circumstances, a Ferrari with a £50,000 loan against it was hardly a big asset. On top of that, I knew that once the new Flat season came around, running my racing operation would incur large additional costs. My personal and business outgoings would total around £3,000 per week.

Throughout the winter, I'd assumed that when the season approached I would bounce back to life and become the active-minded, positive person I had been before. I had planned to start work in early March, but when the moment arrived I really struggled. I was so deeply depressed, in such a rut, that just sitting at a desk proved very difficult. The agents I had used to place bets for me in the past were ready and waiting for action, so I needed to produce some results. But I lacked confidence. I'd always had the ability to beat the bookmakers, but now I was coming back after nearly a year off. None of the form since June 1998 meant anything to me, and I had forgotten virtually all the form before that. I had never tried betting without this knowledge and had no idea whether it would work. It was likely that I would regain the thread at some stage, but at the rate that my assets were dwindling I could easily go bust before that happened.

My situation was desperate. The psychological effect of knowing I was not many losers from going under terrified me. The previous eight months had taken me to the edge of my sanity and now circumstances were forcing me to run along that cliff edge. In the end, I had no choice but to take the plunge. The brave thoughts I'd had about my comeback had long disappeared. I was facing the moment of truth.

CHAPTER 7

THE COMEBACK

March 25, 1999. The first day of the turf Flat season.

SOMEHOW, I found a fresh resolve to fight my way out of trouble. It came through channelling my anger into motivation, the motivation to work really hard. I spent time reflecting on what had happened to me and used my resentment to spur me onwards. Using anger as my motivation wasn't a sound method for the long term but, in those first few months, it was the only solution I could find.

I took on an enormous workload. Only sleep and excursions to the gym were allowed to interrupt my schedule. I was toiling away for more than 100 hours a week, watching the racing obsessively, taking notes, talking to contacts and studying the form hour after hour. Looking back, my work didn't have nearly the same precision that it does today. Since then I've learned to pick my moments carefully, focusing my attention on a smaller number of horses, but at the time I chose to try to absorb everything. Each race would be watched repeatedly for the tiniest of details. I'd produce huge lists of all the horses I thought were better or worse than the bare reading of the form book. I'd update the records of every past race, noting the subsequent performance of each horse. I'd form a list of possible bets and check them endlessly and obsessively from every angle, trying to find various reasons to reject them. Only when I was sure would a bet be placed.

I divided my bets into two categories. Smaller punts, those under £1,000, were Trading Bets. They were usually instances where I lacked total conviction but felt the odds were tempting enough to take an interest. A horse might be 14-1 and, while not entirely convinced of its prospects, I would feel 10-1 was a more accurate reflection of its chance and have a bet. At that time betting tax was nine per cent, and after subtracting that I'd expect to make a profit on these bets, although not a huge one. Trading bets included some occasions when I received a 'hot' phone call, perhaps asking me to place a bet for someone else, and included most multiple and Tote bets. 'Trading' didn't mean that I was buying and selling. This was before the days of exchanges, so the word merely meant that a bet was a routine part of my trade.

My larger investments, of £1,000 and upwards, were known as Full Bets. These were the gilt-edged opportunities where I would place much higher stakes. But how high could I afford to go? The largest bet I'd ever had was the aforementioned £20,000 on Blue Goblin in May 1997. I remembered how life had been much more fun in those days. That spring I had strayed from running my business on strictly professional lines and employed a gorgeous personal assistant called Joanna, who had become much more than that by the time we were at Newmarket watching Blue Goblin wing home. Needless to say, and it's an old story, mixing business and pleasure didn't last long, and I later heard of Jo when she appeared in the papers being romantically linked with Prince Harry.

So much had changed since then. Even if I ever reached that level of confidence again, I didn't have the funds to be able to risk £10,000 on a single horse, never mind £20,000. I'd have to play smaller for the moment and hope that I could build funds up in time. The stage was set for my comeback as a professional punter. This is how I got on.

Week 1 to March 27
I enjoyed a fortunate start from only three days' trading. I was far too nervous to try a full bet at this early stage and decided to restrict my interest to a Placepot perm on the three days of Doncaster. I'd say I

was just plain lucky that I made profits of £7,856.10 and £4,070.63 on the first two days from trading stakes, but I reckoned I deserved a little luck to get me started. I had studied the cards, but my recollection of the form was so vague that I was mostly stabbing in the dark. The stress of it all was frightening. It left me feeling mentally exhausted, and by Saturday night I was shattered. Nevertheless, I kept on working through Sunday and prayed that my luck would hold.

Weekly total +£15,959.13

[Note: It may seem peculiar that my stakes were often very random-sounding amounts. A combination of betting tax and the restrictions placed on my agents meant that I frequently ended up with a stake such as £2,716 when £3,000 was intended.]

Week 2 to April 3

My first full bet, and not a very inspiring start. I placed £1,270 at evens on Tarawan in a Leicester maiden, who started at 8-11 and finished second.

Again, fortunately, the trading bets served me well. The main feature was Fallachan, where a stake of £950 at morning prices produced a profit of £4,701. The profit so far was almost exclusively derived from contacts of mine, as opposed to my own analysis. At the time, quite a number of successful punters would ring me to make use of my team of agents, but my contacts were not always successful and I wouldn't be able to cover my expenses without producing winners of my own. In the years to come, lack of time would force me to dispense with most of the contacts business, as my own analysis became dominant.

Weekly total: +£9,911.55
Running profit: £25,870.68

Week 3 to April 10

Trading bets again did well, but without any highlights. You might imagine that I was in long-deferred high spirits after winning more than £30,000 in three weeks, but I kept the lid on my emotions, all too aware that I was still reliant on the success of hot phone calls from my contacts.

Weekly total: +£6,389.98
Running profit: £32,260.66

Week 4 to April 17

A busy but disturbing week. Despite working almost every waking hour, my full bets were not yet hitting the target, having produced just one winner in four weeks.

Candleriggs, trained by Ed Dunlop, was by far my largest bet of the week with a stake of £7,608.20. I had been very impressed with his win at Kempton that month and received a very strong word for him to follow up in a six-furlong handicap at Newmarket. I averaged better than 4-1 from the morning prices, which seemed fine when he started at 9-4, but he could do no better than sixth. I have never been a fan of Dunlop as a trainer, although my losses on this occasion were a drop in the ocean compared to the sums a runner from his stable would later cost me.

Weekly total: -£6,469.55
Running profit: £25,791.11

Week 5 to April 24

By the end of this week I was beside myself, for a combination of reasons. The overall profit figure looked good but was highly mis-leading, as it failed to take account of £15,000 expenses since the start of the campaign, let alone the huge costs of the winter. After expenses I was up £8,000, but this included two lucky Placepots and good returns from my contacts. My own selections had produced losses.

Then there were my agents who placed bets for me. They'd all put plenty of time into preparing for the season. Not many of them were involved in the Placepots and they probably tended to fare slightly worse than me on the trading bets, perhaps feeling that I should receive the very best of the prices obtained. As most of them had made no money from betting since June, I could hardly blame them for starting to get twitchy. One reported that his right-hand man had phoned to say that he was putting his cue in the rack.

Finding reliable people to put bets on for me has not been easy. I've never had a formal recruitment process, there are no cards in job centres advertising vacancies and I don't really do interviews. Over the years, I've met many people in and out of the business who had an interest in gambling. I've just relied on my instincts and a little research as to who to trust with my money and my confidential betting information. Initially, I'll make a few background inquiries if someone suggests that they become involved. If I receive positive references, I'll try them out with the odd bet here and there, and then check that they have carried out my instructions to the letter. If all progresses satisfactorily they will become occasional agents. Then, if they continue to do things exactly as requested, they may be promoted to full agents.

None of my agents, either part-time or full-time, are paid by me, nor do they receive expenses. They all work on the basis that they will earn enough by betting for themselves alongside my business. I tend to receive a sizeable share of the business done, but expect the agents to make a healthy profit by the end of the year. The number of agents has grown steadily and I've probably used as many as 200 down the years, although most only infrequently. At any one time

I'll be able to call on between five or ten for serious business, with 30 to 40 I can turn to occasionally. In time, main agents usually take on their own team of sub-agents, so that the number of people placing a bet will far exceed the group I deal with directly.

I've often been asked if ensuring my winnings are paid has been a problem. Happily, that's rarely been the case, and with good reason. Once someone's betting fortunes have been transformed from the red into the black, it goes without saying that they are usually pretty keen not to rock the boat.

However, over the years I have had to relieve a number of my agents of their duties. It came as a major surprise to me that after our hugely profitable association, they were willing to queer their pitches by placing bets with banned outlets, the term I use for people or firms who join in with big feet and cause a huge market move or deduce that the bet is mine and leak this to the betting world. I've always been very strict in banning bets to such quarters, yet some agents continued to use them, evidently assuming I wouldn't find out. I invariably did, and that was that as far as they were concerned.

Although only a minority of bets have been placed by my agents through betting shops, they have produced some of the more bizarre incidents. Those in authority at bookmakers' trading centres tend to understand their rules fairly well, whereas sometimes a local shop manager will get a little carried away and try to overstep the mark.

I used to have an agent called George Riding, who toured betting shops for me in various towns and cities. In one town George had taken to flitting between a succession of William Hill shops to avoid detection. After a string of sizeable wins, he was ushered into the back room by one of the managers, who was presumably keen to protect his bonus. He sat the slightly built George in the corner and handed over his winnings with a very stern warning that he was becoming seriously upset with him. He then issued a final warning accompanied with much wagging of fingers. George didn't visit that betting shop again, but I know a few men who did.

Another agent, Richard Lamb, spotted a notice displaying his photo behind the counter of another William Hill shop. They had concluded that he was the most unprofitable customer in the area and circulated what almost amounted to a 'wanted' poster, warning the staff not to accept his bets. It was a little surprising that they failed to place the notice out of sight and, once again, we made the appropriate changes to the team.

Stranger still, one Ladbrokes shop manager chose to make up his own rules after we backed a 14-1 winner in one of their shops. He informed my agent that they were going to settle at the SP of 8-1. It was time for me to take over and have a word with customer services at head office, as this stance had no hope of success if we chose to go to arbitration. I decided to adopt a light-hearted approach. "You're not by any chance a betting man, are you?" I asked. "Because I'm willing to bet you one million pounds against a tenner that this bet will be paid out at 14-1. We can do this the easy way or the hard way, with lots of bad publicity for Ladbrokes. We can also involve the authorities, but let me assure you, your manager is a buffoon and the bet will be paid out at 14-1."

The customer services manager said that he would look into it further and asked for my name. "You can call me Mr Smith, Mr John Smith," I replied, in a tone that indicated they should not expect me to help them any more than necessary. Mr Smith was to call back the next day and find that Ladbrokes had seen sense and would indeed pay out at 14-1.

The redoubtable Mr Smith also sprang into action to deal with an area manager of the Tote, who had not been impressed to find two winning £500 bets at 10-1 placed at different shops in the same town. He seemed to be contemplating a similar course of action to the Ladbrokes manager by paying out at shorter odds. When I reminded him of the rules, he confirmed that the correct payment would follow, but added that he didn't want any more bets from 'you and your people'. Mr Smith's reply was borrowed from a nursery rhyme. I told him: "Well, be advised that I also know the butcher, the baker and the candlestick-maker – and I'll be the one who decides when I've finished betting with you."

Fred Done made a name for himself with a rapidly expanding betting shop empire now called Betfred, and also a telephone betting business. This was launched in the racing papers by large adverts adorned with Fred's beaming smile. His initially brave approach to telephone betting caused speculation in our office as to how long it would take to wipe that smile off his face. No-one predicted a long campaign. Sure enough, inside a year, Fred became more cautious about his telephone operation, and advertisements began appearing featuring a glum-faced proprietor. The smile had disappeared, although this, of course, might just have been coincidence.

We had profitable dealings in one of Fred's Manchester shops, that my agent Derek Brearley targeted with some rather successful multiple bets. Having initially gone behind in his dealings, Derek collected close on £100,000 in a short spree of winners that led to his being moved on as a customer and losing his privileges of tea and toast served by the staff.

When Derek moved house, it seemed an ideal opportunity to reignite his relationship with Fred. However, I thought it wise to alter Derek's appearance, as even in another shop many miles away a high-staking, chubby little bloke would inevitably stand out, and might well be recognised as the man who had already inflicted punishment on Fred in Manchester. So I asked Derek to dye his hair, on the basis that if staff rang head office with news of a guy with bright blonde hair, it wouldn't match up with his previous description. To ensure that Derek chose the right shade, I suggested that he switch on BBC TV's tennis coverage at Wimbledon that fortnight.

"There, you see Sue Barker, you want to go every bit as blonde as that," I suggested, and within hours, his new strikingly blonde hair-style made him resemble a chubby version of Eminem. But, sadly, the new association bore smaller fruits a little too quickly in that betting shop, and Derek never reached 'high staking, tea and toast' status there. Eventually his hair colour returned to normal, via a streaky stage. Some agents are willing to go beyond the call of duty if the profits are rolling in.

And although profit is always the key objective, occasionally I still take a decision for pure entertainment. What's life without a bit of fun? Derek's first name is actually Stephan. Derek is his middle name, but we felt he looked a lot more like a Derek than a Stephan and his name was changed accordingly within the ranks. We tried to be helpful by ensuring that all post was addressed to Derek Brearley and we would even take time out to ensure that his phone's voice-mail message was kept up to date.

For some reason, Derek didn't seem a big fan of this arrange-ment, and was forever using the phrase 'Don't call me Derek'. When I bought a yearling by Sri Pekan for only 5,000gns, it seemed a cheap enough price to take a chance on security and allow a name that might be traceable to me. We registered the name Dont Call Me Derek, ensuring that the man himself was unaware of our little plot. When the horse made his debut, we made sure that Derek was on the phone on some spurious pretext. Suddenly, with commentary on full volume, there were all sorts of expletives coming down the phone – some I'd never heard before. We decided on a policy of blan-ket denial and protested our innocence vehemently, even phoning him back to claim we had checked with the stable that the owner had been referring to another Derek altogether. However, our Derek didn't seem completely convinced.

The following spring, he raised the subject again while a number of agents were having dinner after a day at the breeze-ups. I tried a total bluff and offered Derek a bet of £500 at 4-1 that I had any connection with the horse. I even placed the £2,000 on the table in front of me. Fortunately, Derek assumed that I wouldn't have offered the bet if I was going to lose and turned the bet down, so we were able to prolong the joke. Later in the season, we decided it was time to put him out of his misery. As Derek is a very likeable guy and has a fairly thick Northern accent, we changed his nickname to The Chummy Northerner. After Derek the racehorse won his first race, we changed the partnership name to 'The Chummy Northerners', after which further denials of our involvement were pointless!

Another agent, Bill McClymont, was only part way to recovering a decade of losses when Ronnie, his friendly local bookmaker, who had promised him an account for life, moved him to SP bets only. This seemed harsh, so a plan was devised to supplement recent winnings. I noticed that the August Bank Holiday Monday cards were unusually full of races with long odds-on favourites, so I put together an each-way accumulator, picking a second- or third-favourite that seemed sure to be placed in each race. As long as every selection was indeed placed, the winnings would come to many thousands.

The hapless Ronnie, who happened to be out when the bet was placed, returned from his day trip with one leg of the bet to go, and phoned Bill up to vent his frustration. With a red-hot favourite at 1-4, the reliable-looking 5-1 second-favourite was about 95 per cent certain to be placed, but would pay out at even money for the first three. After it finished second, as expected, Bill's account had hit the front and was then closed down for good. This type of each-way betting can be profitable on occasions but is hated by bookmakers.

Given that the objective is not just to win but to take each outlet for the maximum amount possible before they run scared, it is not something I do very often.

Returning to my present problems, though, the worst part of it was sheer exhaustion, as I had a work schedule that couldn't be sustained for long. The intensity of my work was getting to me, but I had to keep it up. I worked from waking until sleeping on the Sunday, determined to fight back.

Weekly total: -£2,754.95
Running profit: £23,036.16

Week 6 to May 1

Guineas week at Newmarket. After a quiet Monday, I got cracking on the Tuesday with three full bets. One of them, Petit Palais, provided the first five-figure win of the year. I collected £16,461.60 from a stake of £1,863.90. The race he won was only a Nottingham seller but it made a huge difference to my state of mind. You see more horses needing longer distances than shorter when watching racing, but Petit Palais had run a nice race over a mile a week earlier and just looked as if he might win a tiny race back at a sprint distance. So it proved. It was the only race he ever won.

After a few minor setbacks, I had my second decent touch of the week with Achilles Star at Newmarket on the Friday. I'd liked his run at Windsor a couple of weeks earlier, a race that looked very solid, especially as I'd seen hot money for two of the main contenders. I felt he was overpriced at 14-1 and won £23,865 from a stake of £1,635.

Although the trading bets had a week that was both hectic and disappointing, I felt a lot better and a lot more capable, so to speak, because I'd made more than £20,000 from my own selections, with two good-priced winners from ten full bets. However, the wins could do nothing for my exhaustion levels, and I knew that continuing at such an unforgiving pace could last only for weeks rather than months.

Weekly total: +£11,975.06
Running profit: £35,011.22

CHAPTER 8

SECURITY REVIEW

O N THE day that Achilles Star won, I heard the news I had been waiting for. Calvin Hall's murder trial had been scheduled for the autumn. It was time for a full security review with Michael Thornton.

We both now felt that my immediate risk was reduced, and Michael was especially confident about this. Although Hall's accomplice was still at large, we could be certain that preparations for the forthcoming trial would be by far his greatest concern. Allowing for time served on remand, Hall would be able to apply for parole in around a year, whereas a conviction for murder would bring a life sentence. Potential witnesses in the murder trial now had far more reason to be fearful of Hall than I did.

Given these circumstances, Michael decided that security procedures outside London could be relaxed. We decided that my location in London would remain a secret, as if Hall was acquitted, he would be at large in a year or two. But we also decided that I would travel to the races whenever it suited, and enjoy a fair amount of time away from London that way. I would still be very discreet about my travel plans, relying on the fact that the racing community thought I still lived in Cambridge. Hotel bookings would use an old Cambridge address and I would be careful not to take anything with me that revealed my London address.

At the races, I would stay away from the public areas wherever possible, spending most of the time in private boxes or a discreet corner of the restaurant. Of course, I would need to ensure that my trips did not interfere with my workload; I would continue analysing while at the races, as well as back at the hotel room and even when being driven to and from London.

Week 7 to May 8

After nearly 50 days of working flat out, I finally had some serious profit to show for my efforts. A win in a Chester handicap for Enfilade was uplifting, all the more so because there wasn't a single strong reason for the bet. I just felt the horse was a big price and finally found the confidence to have a full bet on my own instinctive judgement without needing a long list of reasons to back me up. I looked upon it as a turning point. My profit was only £12,786 from an each-way stake that totalled £2,180, but I was pleased nonetheless.

On the Saturday, I allowed myself a day at Lingfield in a private box. I was friendly with Martin Green, the racing manager of Pertemps as well as being one of my agents. He had originally contacted me when I ran my tipping service, representing a company that was selling advertising space on SIS, the TV service supplied to betting shops. I had also become friendly with Tim Watts, the Pertemps chairman. They often took boxes at the races, which helped me in keeping a low profile.

A fair-sized bet (£5,102.50) on Presumed was amusing, as Martin obtained a special 'sponsor's' price of 11-4 from the Tote to part of my bet, and we had a chuckle about whether the Tote would extend me long-term facilities at inflated odds. Staying in the box was made to feel less like a restriction as Pertemps, as usual, had a couple of models to lead in the winner. On this occasion one of them was a former Miss Great Britain, Leilani Dowding.

At long last, I had reason to be content with the way the season was progressing, but physically I was beginning to wear out. I was only averaging five hours' sleep a night, and as the number of fixtures each week increased, I found that betting matters were spinning around inside my head until the early hours.

Weekly total: +£51,031.14
Running profit: £86,042.36

Week 8 to May 16

The week began with a trip to Windsor on Monday evening. I felt that Pandjojoe was just about nailed on in the sprint handicap and wanted a really large bet. He had been tremendously impressive when landing a gamble at Newcastle the week before and had only a 6lb penalty to overcome, but, crucially, he had a massive draw advantage as well, being drawn 25 of 25. It was a big field but I couldn't see him being beaten. At fairly short forecast odds it made sense to visit the track, as I wanted to avoid paying betting tax. Every little helps.

Windsor had once been known for the strength of the market on Monday nights, as the course bookmakers stood up to the crowds of City boys betting in size. Although racecourse markets had become weaker in recent years, I was still hopeful of managing a very hefty bet on Pandjojoe. I wasn't keen to place the bet myself, though. The course bookmakers have long made it their business to monitor the activity of the faces that they know, so I'd checked that the Oilman, a trusted contact, was going to be there. I met him behind the stands, away from prying eyes. Pandjojoe seemed to settle down at 9-4 after early trading and I gave the Oilman instructions to take the price. "How much?" he asked. "All of it," I replied. The Oilman looked a little startled, but being a man of few words just wandered off to get to work.

I hoped the market was good for £20,000, with an outside chance of my stake nearing £30,000. I was really confident. When I innocently wandered into the ring, though, I was dismayed to see Pandjojoe's price collapsing. I had to step in urgently to tell the Oilman to take lower odds if necessary, risking my conversation being spotted. He moved in for the 2-1 and 15-8, but after about three minutes the 15-8 had disappeared too, and I had only got £9,000 on Pandjojoe.

The ring seemed to have gathered that I was the source of the money – despite my precautions I had been rumbled. I had mixed feelings after Pandjojoe trounced his field by three lengths.

Interest in on-course betting has declined in recent years, partly because betting tax is no longer saved by attending the races. In some ways this is a shame, as the betting ring was a far livelier place to be when I first went racing. I recall being shocked while still at university when a friend, who was helping me spread a bet on an outsider around the betting ring, overheard the bookmaker say to his clerk, 'He's trading with Veitch'.

At the time, I didn't realise that my activities were being noticed. It taught me that course bookmakers possess the ability to establish quickly which faces might inflict damage upon them. Since then, I've been very careful with on-course activity, rarely betting unless I had unknown faces available and a strong market to work with.

Next day, it was York. I'd studied the card late into the night after getting back from Windsor and one of my fancies was Star Precision at long odds in the mile-and-a-half handicap. Most of owner Bridget Swire's horses favoured soft ground and Star Precision was no exception. It was a big surprise, therefore, when she was written off at 25-1 after running poorly on her first-ever start on fast ground. The Pricewise column in the Racing Post had tipped Star Precision, so time was not on my side if I was to get the best morning odds. I had to make an awful lot of phone calls to manage a stake of £1,500 each-way, mostly at 25-1.

It was to be an entertaining day. William Hill had invited Martin Green to come to their box with a guest, and he couldn't resist taking me along. When we walked in, Martin shook hands with Hills chief John Brown and introduced me. Brown didn't know me by sight but did a huge double-take when told my name, seemingly amazed to find a prominent enemy joining him in the Hills box.

Hills had been one of the firms to offer 25-1 about Star Precision, and after she won the first race by three lengths the two sides were suffering contrasting fortunes. There was a follow-up. I'd combined Star Precision with smaller fancies in some doubles and two trixie bets (three doubles and a treble). Things were clearly running for me when the second leg won at double-figure odds. Some of those doubles were already winning bets, but in the trixies I now had huge stakes running on to Regal Exit and National Anthem in a later race. Regal Exit was the bigger price and stood to win me around £700,000.

The next few minutes were priceless. I was sitting at the back of the box, scribbling away on pieces of paper, working out the various amounts running on in my multiple bets. I had a glass of champagne on the table and, after the second leg had come off, Martin, who had placed some of the bets, walked over to my table and plonked a nearly full bottle next to the glass. He said nothing, just raised his eyebrows and gave a little smirk. Martin knew that I was only a very light drinker at the races. His gesture was more a signal of the way the day was going.

Returning to the balcony, he bumped into Brown, who asked politely how he was getting on. Knowing better than to give anything away, Martin replied: "Oh, not too bad, I think I'm still in the Place-pot. How about you?" "We're a bit concerned, to tell you the truth," Brown replied. There really is no sound quite as beautiful as a nervous bookmaker. "We've little multiple bets running up all round the country and they're all winners so far. They come to a fortune if they all come in." Little did he know that his firm's tormentor was sitting right behind him. "Sounds worrying," said Martin, feigning concern. As the runners entered the stalls for the last leg, I remember Martin saying: "Don't retire, Veitchy, if you get the result here. Think of the troops." There was no danger of my retiring if I scooped the pot. Not after I'd come this far and was just hitting some serious form.

The fairytale ending didn't happen. Not quite. National Anthem came with a strong run inside the final two furlongs only for disaster to strike as his saddle slipped. He still managed to finish a desperately unlucky second, beaten just three-quarters of a length. I was disappointed but remained in good spirits. I'd still made a profit of £65,059.80 from the various doubles, as well as my profit on the Star Precision each-way bet, and it was money that I badly needed. I heard a week or two later that Hills had subsequently twigged who was behind the business, which made me smile all the more about the day in their box. Martin was not invited back the following year.

A loser the next day quickly made a dent in my profits. Golden Snake was a major fancy of mine in the Dante Stakes. I felt that the favourite Slip Stream was a talking horse who had achieved little of substance, while the second-favourite Mutaahab had not impressed me at Newbury on his previous start and I doubted whether he was yet back to his best of the previous season.

As my profits increased, my full bet stakes were also rising very quickly. I staked £18,000 on Golden Snake at around 7-2 and should have collected, too. In a tactical race, his jockey Michael Hills got into all sorts of trouble while the winner Salford Express stole first run. Next time out Golden Snake won the first of four Group 1 races, whereas Salford Express never won again in 15 starts.

On the final day at York I went for another touch, staking £7,720.47 on Marton Moss, who had shaped nicely at Thirsk on his previous start and was well handicapped on last season's form. He ran poorly, for no apparent reason, but went on to win his next two starts. The week ended quietly, and I was happy to balance the figures on the Sunday with very close to £100,000 added to the running profit.

Weekly total: £99,210.20
Running profit: £185,252.56

Week 9 to May 22

A much quieter week. I was extremely tired and had the nagging feeling that my mind was starting to become jaded. I knew I'd set an unsustainable pace. Now it was a case of how much longer I could hold on.

Weekly total: -£7,134.35
Running Profit: £178,118.21

Sunday, May 23

This was another day I would not forget. I'd been invited to the Irish 1,000 Guineas, but it wasn't just any invitation. Tim Watts had hired a World War Two transport plane to fly a group over to the Curragh for the day. The flight was thrilling, if a little less smooth than a modern jet. Provided I worked until the moment I left home and picked up the thread as soon as I got back, I could enjoy a day off, especially as I very rarely bet on foreign racing. I've never seen the benefit of getting too involved in situations where my knowledge of the form is too sketchy.

We had lunch at the course and settled down to watch the racing. Inevitably, after a couple of hours, my mind was on the week ahead. I kept lists of the interesting horses I had identified during the season, and the two who were by far the most interesting, Indian Lodge and Ellens Academy, were set to run over the next three days. The more I thought about it, the more I was sure that this was a major chance to catapult the season forward.

I wandered away from the group. Suddenly, my emotions were running at full strength. I walked up and down with the phrase 'three days in May' going through my head again and again. I kept telling myself that this was my chance to secure everything in just a few days. My comeback, thus far, had netted me about a year's expenses, but here was the chance to get wealthy again.

87

There were tears in my eyes. First time. I'd kept everything hidden inside since June. I'd begun to channel the anger out in March, but only the anger, and now the rest of the emotion was emerging. I walked up and down thinking about everything that had happened and repeating the words 'three days in May'. I was much quieter on the return flight, more composed. Thinking, planning, scheming.

Week 10 to May 29

Monday was spent in the office, endlessly analysing the races in which my two big hopes were entered. I worked late into the night and woke to worrying news. Indian Lodge had been declared for Yarmouth the following day, but the ground was forecast as firm. His win at Newbury had, to my eyes, been the most taking maiden performance of the year, but his stride pattern that day made it clear to me that soft ground would suit him best. He was trained by Amanda Perrett, and I recalled that Martin had met her a few weeks earlier. I asked him to phone Perrett and urge her to consider how notorious Yarmouth was for very firm ground.

In the afternoon, I had an each-way bet on Heartwood in the mile-and-a-quarter maiden at Beverley. She'd shaped like she needed further at Windsor over a mile last time out, and I was surprised to see her at a double-figure price. Her victory put me more than £20,000 in front from the first two of my 'Three days in May', with the fireworks still to come. Time to light the blue touch-paper.

Work started early on Wednesday morning. Ellens Academy was running in a sprint handicap at Newbury that evening and the race had been priced up overnight, which normally made for a strong betting market. Ellens Academy had shown at Carlisle three weeks earlier that he was capable of a far higher rating than he had there, and I couldn't see him being beaten off a mark of only 63. That performance at Carlisle was remarkable, as he finished second despite his saddle slipping soon after the start. Ladbrokes offered 7-1 and, with plenty of other horses being tipped, my agents took everything available at 11-2 or bigger.

That done, my focus switched to a minor contest at Yarmouth and Indian Lodge. Martin had failed to convince Perrett of my concerns about the horse on quick going. The ground was a major worry, but I was convinced I was dealing with a horse who was far too good for any contest at Yarmouth. Moreover, I liked the look of the race. The only credible danger among his five rivals was Zarfoot, who had won the other division of the maiden Indian Lodge landed at Newbury. I was in no doubt that Indian Lodge was the better horse yet, amazingly, most of the pundits showed more interest in Zarfoot.

I bet just over £20,000 after tax on Indian Lodge at odds of around 5-2. On easier ground I'd have played even stronger, but £20,000 was enough on firm. The result was never in doubt. Indian Lodge won by only a neck, but was always cantering and could have won by much further.

I'd knocked off the first one. Now I had to wait a few hours for the evening's entertainment. I would have liked to have obtained more of the morning prices available about Ellens Academy and was wondering whether to move in again as the race approached. The odds had contracted, however, as my business was having an effect on the market. Although two or three points shorter was still a good price in my view, it went against the grain to take a price that I had created by causing earlier odds to tumble.

Mid-afternoon, I received a call that made up my mind. An odds compiler, Barry Beasley, had sent out his lunchtime forecast and had reported that Ellens Academy was 'drawn near Swindon', a reference to him being drawn very low (2 of 21). At the time, a high draw was normally crucial in sprints at Newbury, but on this occasion I was ahead of the pack, because I knew that the course had railed off a section of ground near the stands' rail where the higher-drawn horses would normally race. For once, the low draw was definitely not a negative factor. Beasley, however, was a good judge who was well respected by many bookmakers, including some of those who trade at Newbury. Course bookmakers were inclined to oppose a horse who was short in the betting on the basis of form from a small northern track like Carlisle. Now they would think the draw was a huge problem too, and Ellens Academy's price was sure to drift. Time for a double smash.

A double smash is a term I coined for the rare occasion where I placed as much as possible at morning prices – 'smashed into it' in slang betting parlance – and then took as much as I could later on when the pre-race betting came out. Ellens Academy was available at 6-1 and 11-2 to big money and by the off my bets totalled nearly £20,000. The race proved easy for both of us, as he sped home unchallenged by three lengths.

I'd done it. I was well over £150,000 up on my three days. Looking back, I can't believe I didn't just sit around with a smile on my face all evening. It says something about my mental state that I didn't. Instead, I felt like I'd just won a battle in a long war, and I didn't smile or relax. I fended off a couple of celebratory calls from agents, save for confirming a couple of bets on horses still to run, quickly balanced the day's figures and headed off for some exercise. It's easy to be anonymous at a London gym. People don't talk to strangers. Cannon's Covent Garden had a large underground gym floor and I remember working out there, my mind still racing every bit as intensely as it had all day.

It was the night of the Champions League final. Manchester United were on the way to their famous Treble-winning victory with two goals in the dying seconds against Bayern Munich. Nearly everyone took a break to watch it upstairs, but I just carried on. I remembered how I'd watched the England World Cup game against Argentina alone in a dingy hotel room in June. "Swap with anyone," I'd said. I wasn't going to forget how I felt then; I wasn't ready to take my foot off the pedal, not by a long chalk.

Those three days remain the most memorable betting period of my life. The following year, I bought a yearling by Cadeaux Genereux at Tattersalls sales, named her Three Days In May and put her into training with William Haggas. She wasn't a star, but was backed from 6-1 to 3-1 when winning a little handicap at Thirsk on June 18, 2002, which happened to be the first day of Royal Ascot, almost exactly four years after my troubles began.

I was in roaring form in the office the next day. I had a spare mobile phone for each agent so that I could talk to them all at the same time, usually to co-ordinate a bet. I called them all for a morning briefing, explaining that they would need to find an increasing number of new betting accounts. Having enough outlets to sustain the momentum was vital.

The rest of that week was fairly quiet. I didn't slow my workrate down, but I was reluctant to get too heavily involved for fear of spoiling the most important betting week of my life. I was like a batsman who's just played the perfect cover drive and feels compelled to stay in position for an extra couple of seconds to savour the moment. The week's final decision was that trading bets would now be a maximum of £2,000 in line with my larger stakes for full bets. The year's profit had now leapt to more than £300,000 and I now had real financial security.

Weekly total: £159,876.93
Running profit: £337,995.14

CHAPTER 9

CHANGE OF EMPHASIS

Week 11 to June 5

A COLLECTION of small losses were mostly offset by Manndar, the one big bet of the week. He'd won with a ton in hand at Bath three weeks earlier but the full strength of the performance wasn't clear at the time. In the 24 hours before his run on Saturday, the second and fourth from Bath both came out and recorded markedly improved figures. Had this happened earlier in the week, I suspect that Manndar would have opened at maybe 1-2 for a Listed race at Newmarket. As it was, he was available at even money, and I staked nearly £20,000.

Weekly total: -£1,736.93
Running profit: £336,258.21

Week 12 to June 12

A quiet, losing week between Epsom and Royal Ascot, when much of my time was taken up with research projects. I was keen on Regal Song and Petarga, a pair of sprinters who had shown enough to suggest they would win in their grade; unfortunately, they didn't. I recorded losses of £6,758 and £4,850.50, and closed the week's figures on Saturday afternoon before beginning preparations for Royal Ascot. Each week has to have a cut-off point at which balances are agreed with all the agents.

Weekly total: -£12,411.35
Running profit: £323,846.86

Week 13 to June 20

Royal Ascot week, almost a year after I'd been forced underground. It proved some anniversary. The week's figures below actually started on the previous Saturday evening, with a bigger result than anything I achieved at the royal meeting.

I'd received a whisper for Admirals Flame in a mile handicap at Leicester, and further inspection suggested he was one of very few in the race on a winning handicap mark. He looked like being a big price, but I needed a plan to get the money on in a small race on a quiet Saturday evening. If I moved at early prices the firms would immediately react to the hot money and the odds would tumble. I reckoned that as Admirals Flame was a veteran at eight, they would allow some reasonable bets on him once they had taken plenty of money for other runners, so I decided to leave it as late as I dared before showing my hand. It worked a treat. I managed to get around £3,500 each-way at 16-1 and the bets went on so late that the SP was unaffected. Betting in large amounts rarely goes quite as smoothly as it did that night, but it takes two to tango, of course, and Admirals Flame did his part by finishing with a flourish to land the spoils by a short head.

Four days at Royal Ascot produced losses. In most cases I was just supporting my judgement of the form without any huge edge, but I played in fair size as I'd been going so well. I had to wait until what was then the Ascot Heath meeting on Saturday, when the clothes horses took a back seat, before striking a blow in a Listed contest with Holly Blue. Although the £17,594 winnings weren't huge by my standards, it was an early race and I'd used Holly Blue to kick off various doubles with four other horses – one of whom, Pips Magic, connected at the morning price of 14-1. The double won a little over £30,000, which gave me a healthy surplus from the week's trading bets.

There was also a substantial loser to end the week. Pressurise had looked progressive the year before and, with a very good word that he was ready first time out in a two-mile handicap, I went in. He finished third.

Weekly total: £85,732.28
Running profit: £409,579.14

Week 14 to June 27
The end of Ascot week prompted a vital change of emphasis. My confidence was now sky high, but I felt increasingly exhausted and woefully short of sleep. I knew I had to slacken the pace. Wall to wall racing in high summer, seven days a week, had become too much for me to analyse closely. The solution was to set a cut-off point based on the distance of races, and from now on I'd only work in the fullest detail on races of a mile or shorter. I'd still have mountains of homework, but I'd take a few hours off here and there. Hardly slacking, mind.

Although the next three months would still see me studying harder than at any time outside 1999, the Monday of week 14 marked the end of the most intense period of work I'll ever achieve. I'd channelled my anger to produce a workrate that I couldn't sustain again – nor would I wish to.

I used some of the spare time to enjoy involvement as an owner. Before 1999, I'd owned parts of three horses. Now, in partnership with Tim Watts and some smaller shareholders, I dipped my toe in again with a two-year-old by Prince Sabo in training with Tim Easterby. Tim was keen to promote the Pertemps brand so I decided to choose a name for the colt that included his company name.

At the time, Bill McClymont was one of my top two agents, responsible for running our main account's spreadsheet. He was just a shade tubby in those days and had made the mistake of adopting the title of controller, which I soon pointed out made him The Fat Controller, or FC for short. Bill had a share of the new horse and I told him the name was to be Pertemps Professional. It wasn't until the day of his debut that Bill found out Pertemps FC was named after him.

A busy weekend saw a win for the biggest bet of the week in Fez, who had impressed me with her victory at Redcar a week or so earlier and netted me £16,335. Win some, lose some. Selfish had looked very well handicapped at Newmarket and I invested £7,152.50. She looked sure to win until weakening close home and going under by a head.

Weekly total: £16,922.65
Running profit: £426,501.79

Week 15 to July 3
An uneventful week, with the smallest number of trading bets for some time. Bandanna was the closest thing to a big result. I thought her run at Ascot the time before was a little underrated and she was a decent second at Sandown at 20-1.

Weekly total: -£8,814.06
Running profit: £417,687.73

Week 16 to July 10
The July meeting at Newmarket began on Tuesday, and the previous day I tried and failed to set up a big ante-post touch. Grangeville had gone near the top of my 'interesting' list at Sandown a month earlier. Unusually for him, Kieren Fallon had made far too much use of Grangeville that day, and I was sure that he could have won with

a better-timed challenge. Monday's paper carried the first ante-post betting for Thursday's Bunbury Cup. Grangeville was as big as 12-1, which looked huge to me, but his price was falling even before my agents started to move. I wasn't the only one who thought the book-makers had got it wrong.

I ended up with a disappointingly small stake of £3,161 on Grangeville at 10-1 and 12-1. In one of the season's most competi-tive handicaps, I had hoped for much more, and on the day the price available wasn't big enough for me. Despite my netting a tidy profit it was a little frustrating to see him win comfortably under Fallon, as a potentially huge touch had slipped away. It wasn't the last I'd hear of Grangeville.

Weekly total: £22,214.15
Running profit: £439,901.88

Week 17 to July 17
A quiet week until Saturday. River Times looked to be quite favoura-bly treated in the mile handicap at Newmarket, but there was a twist. The race had little obvious early pace, and River Times was suited by racing close to the leaders. I spoke to his trainer Tim Easterby and suggested it might be a race he could steal from the front. The plan worked to perfection; River Times – 16-1 in places in the morning and backed to win £38,335 – landed a little tickle, returning at 9-1 .

At the time, it all seemed a bit too easy. The prospect of expand-ing into racehorse ownership had the added bonus that most trainers were far too busy to research races and plan tactics in great detail. My ability to point them in the right direction on a few occasions would surely prove invaluable. I was to enjoy many successes as an owner and make serious profits, although it doesn't always prove as simple as it did in 1999. It's one thing for a trainer to see that a plan makes sense, but often quite another for him to convince the man in the saddle of its merits. Even if a rider agrees with his instructions, you still need him to remember his orders if they are given in advance.

That afternoon, I went for a huge touch on Seraphina in the Newbury Super Sprint. In an extremely strong betting heat I managed to stake more than £6,000 to win and some place as well, mostly at 33-1, and stood to win a fraction over £200,000. It was disappointing when she trailed in tenth, but I was more disappointed a month later when she was beaten only a neck, at 66-1, in the Group 2 Lowther Stakes at York. On that showing, she would have won comfortably at Newbury.

Weekly total: £35,758.30
Running profit: £475,660.18

Week 18 to July 24
The week started with a sizeable loser. Alegria had run well in much better grade at York and I thought she had found an easy race at Yarmouth. I went for a touch at 4-1 and 9-2, but she cost me £16,284 as the race turned into a tactical affair that did not suit her. This was to prove doubly costly, as she convinced me that she would win next time granted a better pace. That wasn't to be the case either. Oh well.

Meanwhile, Pertemps FC had had three races. He had been mildly fancied on his third start at Newcastle, when I'd placed a bet of £2,000, but he ran badly, seeming to resent wearing blinkers. However, a subsequent visit to Tim Easterby's stables at Great Habton told a different story. In a home gallop without blinkers, Pertemps FC had easily beaten three stablemates, two of them winners. Tim had only recently taken over the licence from his father Peter, who was with us at the top of the gallop. He doesn't offer his opinions lightly, so when he said, "That's t'best he's worked all year, that", I knew we'd be going for a punt.

Pertemps FC was entered for a seller at Newcastle on the Saturday. Although a few people knew about my connection with Pertemps, I needed to be at the course to impress on our jockey Kevin Darley that he should race as close to the stands' rail as he could manage, to make best use of the considerable draw bias at the time. Kevin needed to work his way across from his draw, six off the rail.

My first priority at Newcastle was to make arrangements for the Oilman to place a couple of bets for me at Ascot. Zucchero was running there in a ladies' handicap only five minutes after Pertemps FC's race, and I felt he was well ahead of the handicapper after an impressive win a week earlier. With my agents likely to be busy, I gave the Oilman my bet of £8,500, which made my total stake on the race £10,000 after a trading bet earlier in the day. The Oilman managed to average 6-1 as Zucchero was backed from 7-1 to 3-1 before being pipped by a short head.

At Newcastle, I needed to combine placing the business on Pertemps FC with making sure I got my instructions across to Kevin. I was in the parade ring with a mobile at each ear, trying not to attract too much attention. Fortunately, the huge crowd covered the view of the parade ring from the nearby bookmakers. I was going full steam on the phones when he appeared, whereupon I suddenly yelled "hold on!" into both mobiles before putting them down to my side.

Later, I was to learn that giving riding instructions required a combination of firmness and courtesy. Jockeys are used to owners who say plenty but know very little about racing, let alone riding tactics. But I was new to this, the adrenaline was pumping and I needed to return to the phones in seconds to complete the business. I'm afraid I must have come across like a sergeant major. Sorry, Kevin.

"Right. You need to miss the break, just a touch, so that you can switch straight across to the stands' rail. WHATEVER HAPPENS make sure you get on that rail. Then STAY ON THE RAIL. Do not under ANY circumstances come off the rail unless it's inside the final furlong."

Kevin looked a little startled, but a firm nod from Tim Easterby was enough to convince him that he should take notice rather than write me off as a lunatic owner. To his credit, Kevin carried out the instructions to the letter. The betting was a little shambolic, though, with one or two mishaps between agents causing some heated words afterwards. Total winnings of just over £30,000 were disappointing after so much work had gone into the planning.

Back home the next day, I was keen to play at Ascot, where the draw bias was again favouring racing against the stands' rail. Draw biases were much more significant then than now, thanks to improvements in both the techniques and equipment for watering. I fancied Frankie Dettori's mount Cretan Gift quite strongly in the sprint handicap from his favourable position in stall two, and in a strong market got plenty of cash on at 11-1 and 10-1. Frankie was well versed in the value of staying on the rail at Ascot at the time and he swooped through on Cretan Gift to win well.

For the second time, I enjoyed a winning week of almost exactly £100,000. On this occasion it was no coincidence, as I had a couple of bets planned late on Sunday afternoon but, having updated my figures, decided to leave them alone to preserve the six-figure win. I felt it would give me even more confidence going into Goodwood week. It proved a lucky move as I saved £4,000 when both horses lost, but in truth I seriously look down on this sort of profit watching, as betting decisions need to be taken purely on their merits.

Weekly total: £100,134.71
Running profit: +£575,794.89

CHAPTER 10

AYR GOLD CUP

Week 19 to August 1

I HAD arranged to go to Glorious Goodwood with a team of agents, taking the usual care with my travel arrangements. They were all in top spirits and I took advantage of the mood to amuse the team by giving them all military ranks. We had Major Geoffrey Pooley, Major McClymont, Captain Green and, with great reluctance and modesty, I decided that I should be appointed Field Marshal. Major Pooley wasn't terribly keen on the ranking system and opted instead to refer to me as Captain Mainwaring, but such insubordination was ruthlessly squashed.

I dismissed objections to the lack of generals, colonels and brigadiers by pointing out that this gave them all something to aim for, and that a four-rank gap seemed about right for the moment. Our newest agent, Derek Brearley, started out with the rank of private, although his tendency at the time to treat drinking as an alternative to sleeping caused a number of temporary demotions to the rank of cadet.

One agent, Peter Hurst, seemed almost too keen on the ranking system. Initially appointed a Captain, he seemed genuinely serious in seeking promotion to Major as soon as possible. He made sure that my every need was catered for, so I only had to drop a hint for him to be straight on the phone to his Sergeant. "The Field Marshal needs a paper with tomorrow's runners in it STRAIGHT AWAY." He'd have made someone a lovely wife.

Peter had known the legendary punter Alex Bird and was the last man to assist him with his bets. For me, Bird's reputation was somewhat undermined by the fact that much of his winnings came from betting on the results of photo-finishes. Two people subsequently told me that he had a source signalling from the judge's box, which may help explain his astonishing success in that sphere. His autobiography was an interesting collection of tales. The son of a bookmaker, he was an early convert to the benefits of race-time analysis, particularly for two-year-olds, and profited accordingly. He also revealed that he made only 1.83 per cent profit on his turnover, although he had to cut right back and change his methods once betting tax of four per cent was introduced. At one time he was turning over in excess of £2 million a year, which was a lot of money 40 years ago or more, but betting tax curtailed his activities to such an extent that his turnover did not exceed £250,000 in later years. Unfortunately, his former associate Major Hurst became a little too keen on the after-race socialising a couple of years later and proved more than I could handle.

Over the next year or two, as I started to have more horses in training, some of the trainers joined in the rankings banter. I can remember Nigel Tinkler calling me straight after a punt had been landed. Rather than discussing the race, or future plans for the horse, his first words were: "What rank am I now?"

Staying overnight at the races posed a serious danger to my profitability unless things were organised very carefully. Experience taught me that work in hotel rooms was much less effective than that at home, as I didn't have everything around me, so my new assistant Charles Robarts (aka The Robot) would simply recreate my office in the largest hotel room we could find. I would travel directly to the races and my office would then be set up during the afternoon. The idea was that I could work right up to the minute I left my office in London and restart the moment I entered the hotel room. The Robot quickly became a key member of the team, so that it was not long before he had his own assistant to take care of such matters.

On the Monday before Goodwood, I picked up some warm business for an unraced two-year-old called Magical Millie. I felt her three rivals at Folkestone were so moderate that I had to go for quite a punt. Magical Millie lived up to her name when giving me the ideal start to the week with an early bonus of £37,930 from a stake of £10,050. There were no full bets on Tuesday, but a trading bet on Rudi's Pet won me just over £10,000.

Although I was seeing the form well, I was happy to concede that I was in one of those spells when the dice were rolling my way. By Wednesday, my luck was definitely in, as I'd had a five-figure result for five days running. I'd decided that Bachir was a potential star after his first race at Chepstow, where he had been awesomely impressive, and was keen to get stuck into him in a sub-standard-looking Richmond Stakes. I had hoped for odds of 7-4 but had to take less, getting most of my money on at 11-8 and collecting £28,625 for an outlay of £20,000. Now I was finally due some fun. I'd just started seeing a girl called Kryssy, who arrived, looking stunning, for a couple of days. I'd met her through Martin's wife Rebecca, who ran a modelling agency. My workrate dropped until Thursday evening (although I couldn't say the same for my heartrate), and it was good to relax.

By the end of the week, though, I realised that I'd have to be careful not to become carried away with recent successes. My mental state was in some ways still finely balanced, and this brief taste of the high life was in danger of having too much of an effect before I'd had a chance to calm down and reflect on the year. Although huge confidence in my betting skills was a good thing, there was a 24-hour period at the end of the week when I lost my sense of perspective. It cost me dear. By Friday afternoon, when caution was called for, I was so pleased with myself that I allowed self-confidence to get the better of me.

The race concerned was Saturday's Stewards' Cup, the thrilling cavalry charge across the roof of Sussex. I'd decided that Pepperdine, winner of the William Hill Trophy at York, was a Group horse in the making. I had backed him ante-post but knew I had to wait for the draw before I really let rip on the day. I wanted the highest draw possible, and 25 of 30 was fine. To make absolutely sure, I had to ensure that connections knew the importance of racing tight on the far rail.

I didn't know Pepperdine's trainer David Nicholls, but Peter had met him. As I discussed the race among the troops on Friday afternoon, I asked him to find Nicholls so I could let him know my thoughts. This was the point that I should have realised I was getting carried away. Captain Hurst was urgently pursuing his promotion, so he marched straight off. Less than 20 seconds later, to the amazement of all concerned, he marched back into the restaurant with his arm around a slightly bemused-looking Nicholls. After briefing him about the finer points of my views, I brushed aside the comments of a couple of my agents to the effect that he hadn't seemed to be that confident. As for looking bemused, that hadn't done Kevin Darley any harm at Newcastle. Such things didn't matter. Pepperdine was going to win.

I also talked the race over with Duncan Lipscombe, a very sound judge with whom I have often discussed form over the years. He didn't fancy Pepperdine at all. I told him he was wrong. Later, a second losing bet on Alegria in two weeks failed to dampen my enthusiasm, even though the further loss of £13,739.45 made her the most expensive horse of the year to date. If those clues were not enough to set the alarm bells ringing, then a call the next morning should certainly have put me off. The caller told me he'd heard a rumour that the course had been watered unevenly on Friday evening to offset the draw advantage of the far rail. Pepperdine's high draw suddenly didn't seem so comforting.

Now I had three reasons to doubt a horse who was a hot favourite, but by this stage there was no stopping me. I ploughed into Pepperdine all morning and by lunchtime I'd staked more than £40,000. I got the result that my overconfidence deserved – Pepperdine finished 18th.

The only positive that emerged from this sorry saga is that my pig-headed foolishness dawned on me very quickly. I was fuming, and knew I'd been unwise to get so overconfident. I'd had a winning week and was now nearly £600,000 up in four months, so it was hardly a perilous situation. But I had learned a harsh lesson, having wasted more than £40,000 on a horse whose defeat was foreseeable. From that point on, the size of my bets wouldn't be dropping, but I'd always have my foot near the brake pedal ready to press hard when needed.

Weekly total: £23,784.20
Running profit: £599,579.09

Week 20 to August 8
With the Pepperdine disaster uncomfortably fresh in my mind, perhaps I should have pulled in my horns. Instead, I had a losing week, caused largely by a bet of £18,748 on Common Place, who ran a shocker at Newcastle.

Weekly total: -£30,605
Running profit: +£568,974.09

Weeks 21 & 22 to August 22
I combined two weeks' betting into one set of figures to make sure I had time to attend York's Ebor meeting. The only real point of interest in the whole fortnight was an academic one, featuring the shortest price I took all year. While at York, I backed 2-7 shot The Tatling at Brighton, laying out £7,000 for a profit of £2,000.

I'm often asked whether I prefer horses at short or long odds. In theory, it makes no difference to me, as I'm only looking for a horse who's hugely underestimated by the betting market. Now you'll ask how can a 2-7 favourite be seriously underestimated? Only if I think he's 90 per cent sure to win, even allowing for everything that can go wrong in a horse race. I probably back around five odds-on shots a year but I make a profit on that business. The Tatling had the look of a certainty that day. He was outstandingly the best horse in the race and looked sure to give his running. Everything was in his favour and he actually returned at 1-4. I'm not going to get rich with those five odds-on bets a year, but in the course of a season's work they will come along anyway, and I might as well have the profit they make.

You see all sorts of gamblers at the racecourse. That day I was with two agents waiting for the betting to open in the racecourse betting shop. After I had sent them off to take the 2-7, a nearby punter, who overheard our conversation, sprinted away to place his bet. Afterwards, he came rushing up to one of my agents and shook his hand with great excitement. None of us could believe that anyone would be so delighted at backing a 2-7 winner. Times must have been hard!

Fortnightly total: £5,107.45
Running profit: £574,081.54

Week 23 to August 28
A fairly quiet week, with a frustrating run of three seconds balanced by a modest win on Nice One Clare at Newmarket. She would later get well and truly in my bad books when fortunate to beat my big touch horse, Ellens Academy, in the 2001 Wokingham Handicap at Royal Ascot.

Weekly total: £8,655.35
Running profit: £582,736.89

Week 24 to September 4

We enjoyed the day at Beverley on the Sunday, when Pertemps FC looked likely to run well from a good draw. It's interesting how often the draw was a feature of my betting in those days, something that would change radically as watering systems improved over the years. My agents turned out in force, although the eventual bet was only of trading size as his form was looking more exposed by then. The success of my tactical advice about some of Tim Easterby's horses meant that there was no concern about my instructions not being followed by jockey Lindsay Charnock. I wanted him to stay tight against the far rail, be patient and not strike until inside the final furlong. He timed it perfectly on Pertemps FC, who swept into the lead just before the line for a head success.

This caused much hilarity at the yard the next day. Charnock was a strong, extremely effective jockey but not known for holding his mounts up very often, so the lads at Easterby's had much to say about his new ice-cool riding style. I won a little over £12,000 and enjoyed seeing the tactics pay off.

We hurried around Beverley that day like we were in a Benny Hill sketch, trotting off to all points of the track in Indian file. We were late for lunch and had to dash to the paddock, then scampered off to watch the race before heading for the winner's enclosure and being taken off for a drink. Then we darted to the Tote shop, arriving with four furlongs left to run to see Common Place land a small bet at 8-1. The troops cheered the two winners noisily, which was rather embarrassing, as I always prefer to keep my cards much closer to my chest. The following year, the matter of keeping our business confidential became so important that the cheering would have to stop, but it was all a bit of fun at the time.

I'd been very impressed with Jailhouse Rocket at Carlisle the previous week and couldn't see him being beaten at Ripon on the Tuesday.

The need to save the tax on a short-priced favourite made the trip to the track worthwhile and I devised a plan to have the troops spread our cash among a few key layers, but Jailhouse Rocket failed to take off, finishing second and costing me £11,000. I also had a good crack on Brecongill Lad at Epsom on Saturday but he couldn't get past the front-running Tuscan Dream. Goodbye to another £11,118.

Weekly total: -£13,922.10
Running profit: £568,814.79

Week 25 to September 11
It was clear from my profit and loss column that things had slackened off markedly, with no overall progress in six weeks. There were plenty of near-misses, but looking back it's obvious that I was already past my best for the season. The incredible effort I had put in over the first four months had left its mark.

I made a brief visit to the Doncaster St Leger meeting for a couple of serious bets. I underestimated Swallow Flight when going for a £16,000 punt on Desert Knight, who was well beaten in second, but Distant Music was the top two-year-old on my list following his debut and he made no mistake in the Champagne Stakes, netting me £30,172.70. Clive Brittain's stable has never been my favourite, but I had a little tickle on his filly Teggiano, who looked overpriced in the morning betting in the May Hill Stakes. She won by three lengths and I collected £17,274.

Weekly total: £26,297.20
Running profit: £595,111.99

Week 26 to September 18
This week capped my comeback nicely. On Tuesday, I had the best

result of the year from a trading bet on a single horse. My touch on Sharoura was mostly about the draw. Morning odds of 25-1 were just too big about a horse with a plum draw of 14 of 14 at Yarmouth, as the fastest ground was sure to be under the stands' rail, although I wasn't confident, hence my modest trading stake. She started at 20-1 and, no doubt aided by the draw, burst through late on to snatch the spoils by a head. I felt a little fortunate to win £34,645.70 on a minor fancy but it was a great start to the week.

I then made my first visit to Ayr for the Western meeting, although I was to see a lot more of the place over the next few years. Pertemps FC was favourite for the first race on the Friday, but I made a mistake in having a sizeable bet. His win at Beverley had been boosted when the runner-up Mrs P went on to win the Flying Childers at Doncaster, but the overall quality of the form was ordinary at best and I paid insufficient attention to the fact that we'd raced on the quickest part of the track. I was carried away by the exuberance of ownership and saw only the positive side. As with Pepperdine at Goodwood, I learned my lesson quickly and would in future set the bar much higher before I'd back one of my horses.

The money wasn't gone for long, though, as I got it all back and more half an hour later at Newbury. Veil Of Avalon had found a race in which I wanted to oppose all her opponents and she won me £26,435 from bets at 4-1 and 7-2. We placed the business while having an excellent lunch in Ayr's Western House restaurant, a meal most memorable for the fact that one of our group had brought his sister. Halfway through lunch, we noticed that she had the words 'BITE ME' tattooed in huge letters on her lower back. Major Hurst couldn't wait for the end of the day, so that he could say goodbye and add: "I'm sorry I didn't get to bite you, but there's always next time."

And then along came our old friend and Bunbury Cup winner Grangeville. I'd kept my eye on him since July; he'd been beaten

twice over seven furlongs, but those runs taught me that he was definitely going to be best as a sprinter. Soon after the weights came out
for the Ayr Gold Cup I stepped in with a thick bet at 20-1 and 16-1.
He then ran a stormer when third in a Listed race over six furlongs
at Newmarket in late August. I knew that a stronger pace would suit
him even better and I felt he was primed for the Ayr Gold Cup on the
Saturday, so I stepped in again. In all, I backed him to win more than
£130,000, a new record for me.

The day itself was quite an occasion. We stayed at the Turnberry
Hotel throughout the meeting and many hotel guests were invited
for a drink in the box of the well-known ex-trainer Tony Collins, who
had been an integral part of the Gay Future sting at Cartmel, a coup
that is part of racing folklore. We'd decided to watch the big race
from the balcony, but I'd told the troops that I wanted no shouting,
as I was increasingly keen to keep my business under wraps. Silence
prevailed until the two-furlong pole, when Captain Green was unable to restrain himself from yelling "Come on Kieren!"

Martin's vocal support proved the trigger for the rest of the
troops to start shouting for Grangeville, and the noise from the balcony must have accounted for half that on the whole racecourse, as
the horse we had all supported held on after leading a furlong out.
It was a fantastic result, but even as we celebrated I knew I'd have to
work a lot harder on crowd control. Major McClymont was slightly
embarrassed by the loudness of the group after one of the few other
people on the balcony had said a quiet 'well done' and pointed out
that he owned the runner-up, Evening Promise.

Bomb Alaska looked like he'd been laid out for the Ayrshire Handicap but finished second, costing me £12,616.75. It was a race I would
become familiar with, as it would be 2002 before the race was next
won by a horse I didn't own. We stayed at the Turnberry that night
and after dinner had an 'audience' with the great Peter Easterby. We

managed to get him talking at length about his days training top-class jumpers Night Nurse, Sea Pigeon and Alverton, and it was a great end to a memorable week.

Weekly total: £152,438.15
Running profit: £747,550.14

*   *   *

Sunday, September 19 was a day for reflection. After half a year's betting, I'd gone from needing rapid loans to a profit of almost three-quarters of a million. For the first four months of the season I'd worked harder than I'd known was possible, and the pace had still been tough after that. Now it was time to relax. I needed to bring my mind back to a normal state and introduce some balance into my life.

I'd completed the first and most important phase of my comeback. In reality, I'd started my life again, and was not the most levelheaded person at the time. My relationship with Kryssy soon came to an end after I declined her suggestion that she move in with me, a decision I swiftly regretted. Our parting was a heavy blow, and there were a number of evenings when friends were under firm orders to help me drown my sorrows. It was suddenly clear to me that life wasn't as easy as I'd begun to believe, and it would take a little longer before I managed to find the perfect blend of a lifestyle that fitted in comfortably with the strains of making my fortune by gambling.

I continued working until the end of the Flat turf season, but at a vastly reduced level, and even enjoyed some time off. When the turf season ended, I just kept the betting ticking over when I received a strong message for a horse on the all-weather, or for the very occasional jumper. I did have a few losing weeks, but the figures below don't show them. As the amount of business was much smaller, I tended to wait until I was in profit before balancing them. Permit me this minor indulgence!

At the time, I didn't know whether this level of profitability could be achieved again, as the workload wasn't sustainable over a longer term. Fortunately, I became wiser as a punter and delegated as much of the background work as possible. In time, I would create an office structure in which only the studying of videos and form would be my responsibility. Research would be delegated or computerised, and dealing with agents and almost all aspects of trading would be handled by my team.

As it turned out, I was to smash this profit figure in the future, with two consecutive years when I broke the £2m barrier. I enjoyed it all, but none of it would ever give me quite the satisfaction of my comeback in 1999.

19 September – 31 December 1999

Two weeks ending 3 October:	+£60.80
Two weeks ending 17 October:	+£19,190.70
Three weeks ending 6 November:	+£31,762.87
Four weeks ending 4 December:	+£10,581.93
Four weeks ending 31 December:	+£5,789.25
TOTAL 1999 PROFIT/LOSS	**+£814,935.69**

CHAPTER 11

AFTERMATH

HOW did things pan out back in Cambridge over the next few years? Calvin Hall was found not guilty over the killing of Adam Fraser. This was a huge blow at the time. I'd waited more than three years for the certainty that his life sentence would bring, and now he was off the hook. He was released in 2001.

I sustained myself with the knowledge that Hall had seen prosecution witnesses testify against him when on trial for Fraser's murder. Many of these witnesses had known him well, whereas I hadn't known him at all. It seemed logical that Hall would have a far bigger grudge against those people, although this didn't provide any guarantees.

I remained cautious, still used a false name in London, and ensured that very few people knew I lived there. The racing industry still thought I was based in Cambridge. I told friends from Cambridge that I'd settled in the Manchester area. My mail was still sent to Cambridge, then forwarded by the post office to another local address from where someone would collect it for me. In time, when I believed it safe to do so, I told a few more people the story of what had happened. Some laughed and some cried. Some wanted to get to know me a lot better, whereas others preferred to keep their distance. Apart from the odd lapse, they all did their best to respect my security.

As time passed, I came to accept that being careful about my own security issues was part of my life. It was only in 2004 that a breakthrough finally came, although unfortunately it sprang from near-tragedy in someone else's life. Hall and an accomplice were arrested

Left: Cricket, rather than racing, was my childhood sporting obsession. My first few bets were on cricket but I soon switched to racing as it is much more difficult for the bookmakers to price up accurately.

Below: I didn't grow up with horses but this photo comes from a rare day's pony trekking in Wales with my brother Jonathan. As I recall my pony and I collided with a lamppost a few furlongs from home.

Above: My parents John and Norma.

Below: The Veitch brothers looking unusually formal in an early school photo. Jonathan tended to be rather more popular with the teachers than I was and went on to be head boy. My tendency to do the minimum amount of work that I could get away with even led to a sixth form maths prize being cancelled when I was the only plausible winner.

Making a living out of beating the odds

By MALCOLM HEYHOE

WHEN Patrick Veitch first backed horses, £10 was a big bet. Today he backs in four-figure sums.

He's one of racing's leading professionals, operating a premium-rate line of the same name, and turning over three to four hundred thousand pounds a year in bets alone.

At the age of 23, it is a considerable achievement. Veitch has journeyed a long way from his sixth-form days in Halifax, when racing first attracted his interest.

"I was bored with doing my maths A-levels, so I started disappearing into betting shops in the centre of town.

"I spent my evenings, till quite late at night, and often early in the mornings, teaching myself about the various types of races and the ins and outs of form. I learnt fast."

Before he went to read maths at Cambridge, Veitch was already running a small selection service with the help of a friend and one of his customers was David Mitchell of Turfcall, who asked the young Veitch to operate an 0898 service.

"The Professional" phone line was launched in 1989 and four years later the venture has expanded to an office in Cambridge with SIS beamed in. It costs £90,000 a year to keep the show on the road.

"That is an awful lot of money that needs to come in to run the operation but backing horses on a professional basis and advising go hand in hand.

"In 1992 65 per cent of the money I made was from backing horses, 35 per cent came from the telephone lines."

Veitch is serious about

same time, but I might use 15 to divide a bet into a couple of hundred per person.

"They do it because they want to know what I'm backing. This way though, more money goes on a horse than if I laid the bet directly."

He added: "I cannot bet serious money within the Big Three. One account is closed, on another I can only have SP on certain horses as long as I don't come on just before the off and with the final one, if I have a bet, the price is changed."

In the past three years Veitch has landed one big touch and narrowly missed another.

"The biggest touch I had was Dayjur in the Temple Stakes at Sandown during his three-year-old career.

"Looking closely at his form, I knew I could ignore his earlier defeats. He opened at 10-1 and I had all my money on at 10's and 8's, and including my place money I won around £22,000.

"The biggest touch I had that went down was Mighty Mogul in this year's Champion Hurdle. I backed him at 33's, 25's, 20's, 12's and stood to win £53,000. In the words of the trainer on the day, he would have been a 2-1 on shot if he'd got there. A near miss."

Operating as a professional backer separates Veitch, he believes, from the majority of premium rate services as well as giving him an edge over newspaper tipsters.

"I back horses to make a living. That is the major difference between me and the average tipster on a newspaper. On my 0891 number, if

Above: Early profile in *The Sporting Life*.

Below: *The Daily Mail* report on my Scoop 6 win.

Mr Ice-cool's solo strategy

Professional gambler Veitch hits the Scoop6 jackpot with Bonus scheme

Teeton's return delayed for at least two weeks

Profile in *The Telegraph*. Joanna Davies, my PA and girlfriend at the time, briefly hit the headlines a few years later when photographed in an embrace with Prince Harry.

The man who bets for a living – and wins

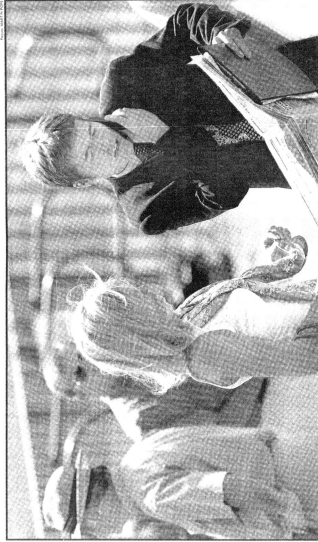

Picture: MARTIN POPE

Today millions will be lost on the Derby – but that's not the kind of gambling that has brought the good life to Patrick Veitch.

By **Lynne Greenwood**

LAST July, Patrick Veitch planned a £15,000 bet on a horse called Dazzle at Newmarket. The day before the race he changed his mind after the horse suffered a well-publicised injury. "I watched the race and it won by a long way at twice the price I was going to invest," he says. "My emotion controlling system was turned to maximum after the race — I was bouncing off the ceiling."

It is not difficult to imagine any punter reacting that way. But Veitch is no ordinary punter, nor a man to reveal his emotions easily. He makes his living from betting on horses.

Above: Pertemps FC lands a gamble at Newcastle in July 1999 and sets the ball rolling for an increase in ownership.

Below: Great News wins his second race in as many days at the 2000 Ayr Western meeting (© John Grossick).

Above and right: Dim Sums adds to a media frenzy when providing Frankie Dettori with his second winner from two rides on his comeback day on 5th August 2000, following his horrific plane crash earlier in the summer. As ever, Dettori's post-race summary was crisp and to the point, answering every question before it was asked. I'd bought Dim Sums after he'd impressed me when winning at Pontefract a month earlier. He ended the season by winning the £150,000 Redcar Two-Year-Old Trophy (© above Paul Webb, left Sean Dempsey).

Above: Itsanothergirl, backed from 20-1 to 5-1, ploughs through the mud in atrocious weather at Haydock in 2001 (© Alan Wright).

Below: Prince Cyrano underlines the edge from my timing methods at the 'breeze up' sales, winning the race for graduates of the sale by five lengths (© Lesley Sampson).

Above: At the races.

Below: Appearing on Channel Four's The Morning Line.

for the attempted murder of a policeman following a stabbing incident. The officer was wounded extremely badly.

At the beginning of December, I made contact with the police to ask the big question. What was the chance that they finally had their man? "Don't worry, Patrick, we've definitely got him this time," I was told. Not only would the victim be there to testify, but Hall had been arrested on the run.

It was distressing that another man had to be so badly injured before Hall was finally brought to justice. I was now one step from freedom, but that last step was important. Despite the CID's confidence, I needed a conviction to be confirmed before being able to relax completely, but the cloud that had hung over me for so long had finally begun to lift. Although I still carry a deafening panic alarm, it's a comfort to know that I'm extremely unlikely to ever need it, but that day I went out without one for the first time in six years.

I spent that Christmas with my parents, visiting my brother Jonathan in Hong Kong. As we enjoyed lunch outside on a warm Christmas afternoon, Jonathan asked everyone to nominate their best day of the year. I assumed there would be no need to ask me, but he did. I replied in that slow questioning voice people use to imply that the answer was really obvious. "The – day – the – guy – was – arrested."

My family seemed surprised at my answer, which shocked me but pleased me too, as I'd evidently been able to successfully shield them from the magnitude of my problems, a course I'd undertaken to protect their security. My answer to my brother's question was the first real hint to them of the extent of the ordeal I had been through.

The case against Calvin Hall finally came to court in 2005. The progress of court proceedings could be tracked on the internet, and it was a Friday afternoon when I saw that the jury had returned. I could phone the court to discover the verdict. I left three of my staff working in my flat and walked away through the hustle and bustle of Piccadilly Circus, an area where I could be totally anonymous. I had gone into this on my own and I was coming out on my own. The lady on the phone confirmed the guilty verdict. The nightmare was finally over. It would be a couple of months before Hall was sentenced to 25 years in jail, but the verdict was enough.

It had taken seven years, so I divided up my friends and had seven big nights out to celebrate. None of the nights finished early.

There was one final postscript. Jerome Davies, who had brought the trouble to my door in the first place by putting Calvin Hall in contact with me, knowing full well the type of person he was, finally got his comeuppance. In 2005, he was jailed for fraudulently altering the mileage of cars. His masquerade of being a successful businessman was further exposed in 2006, when his convictions included benefit fraud. It couldn't have happened to a nicer guy.

PART TWO

PROFESSIONAL PUNTER AND OWNER

CHAPTER 12

SCOOPING THE SCOOP6

I N this section, I've detailed some of the interesting tales and results from the years that followed my comeback, before taking a sabbatical at the end of 2006. Rather than revisiting the diary format I've grouped the years together and discussed firstly my biggest wins and losses, before then running through the stories from those years as a large-staking owner.

As I said at the beginning of this book, details from 2005 onward are more sparingly supplied to avoid giving too much away about my current activities, although I've included the major highlights. It goes without saying that every punter recalls the stories of winners most vividly. Of course, there are many losing days as well, although I've saved the story of my worst losing run – £400,000 in total losses – for part three, when I discuss the mental side of being a professional punter.

My winter break after the comeback season provided an unexpected and highly rewarding diversion in the shape of a massive dividend from the Tote Scoop6. This initially involved picking the winners of a selected six races on a Saturday. All those sharing the winners' pool then have the chance to try to pick the winner of an extra race the following Saturday to scoop an additional bonus.

The attraction for me and other serious players was the rollover. If the main pool and/or the bonus pool were not won, the funds would rollover to the next payout. That winter, the bonus had not been won for many weeks, and by February 2000 a fund of £1.5 million had accrued. This meant that I could invest in the certain knowledge that the odds were in my favour. On February 5, a day the main bet looked achievable, I had a large perm consisting of a few thousand £2 lines. My sole intention was to get a bonus ticket and play for the rollover bonus pool the following week. A few of my agents and friends had been urging me to become involved, so I let them buy into my bet, and in the end about a third of my stake was owned by these third parties.

Results went our way and all six legs were successful, with Red Marauder, hero of the heavy-ground 2001 Grand National, one of the winners. The results were a little too predictable, however, as 18 other players shared the pot, making the profit on the first Saturday a not-particularly-big £8,442.50. Now I had a lot of competition for the bonus fund.

My immediate reaction was that some of the ticket-holders should join forces to maximise the chances of winning the bonus pool. This would involve a number of ticket-holders agreeing privately that they would each go for a different selection and split the winnings if any of them won. The Tote would be sure to pick as tough a bonus race as they could, so being able to cover quite a number of selections would provide a good chance of the group winning the bonus. But there are pitfalls and complications to such an arrangement, and over the next few days I would become intimately acquainted with most of them.

I contacted the *Racing Post* on the Sunday to tell them I was interested in forming a syndicate. The big pools in the Scoop6 had attracted plenty of publicity, so it was a story they were keen to follow. Later that day it emerged that a group of Post staff had a bonus ticket as well. On the Monday, a story appeared in the Post, headlining the fact that I was suggesting a syndicate. The first warning sign, however, was that punters were asked to contact the newspaper, where one of the writers, Simon Turner, had a share in their bonus ticket and had been appointed to run the syndicate. From this point on, matters proceeded out of my control. Simon acted very professionally throughout, but two key decisions made by the group were not to my liking.

The first issue was the number of members in the syndicate. I heard from another contact at the newspaper that Simon had been told he could not refuse anyone admission to the syndicate. Ouch. This was far from ideal. The problem regarding the ideal number of members is very much a mathematical one, which depends on the number of runners in the bonus race and also whether the betting is wide open or dominated by just a few horses. Based on the maximum field sizes for the TV races that Saturday, it seemed likely that we would be talking about an 18-runner field. I calculated that a syndicate of about ten members was ideal, as I felt with careful picking this would allow an 85-90 per cent chance of selecting the winner. There would be a strong possibility of no other ticket-holder sharing the pot if the winner was not in the first three in the betting.

The policy at the Post was to include as many people as possible, on the basis that if everyone joined, the syndicate would split the whole pot. Not only did I prefer to gamble with a syndicate of ten, rather than split the pot 19 ways, but if nearly everyone joined, say 16 out of 19, it was mathematically about the weakest position possible. If the favourite won and was picked by the other three ticket-holders, the syndicate members would each receive only $1/64^{th}$ of the pot.

The second issue was ensuring that everyone got paid. The Tote did not like the idea of syndicates. They wanted to publicise one large individual winner, preferably of over £1m, as this would encourage new punters to participate in the future. As a result, they were not willing to split the winnings themselves, and would send the cheque to whichever member of a syndicate picked the winner. This could create all sorts of problems, not least the possibility of the recipient hightailing it to Mexico with the whole £1.5m, never to be heard from again. This eventuality could be offset by signing documents, although these would be by no means fireproof, as gambling debts are not enforceable in law. Security could be improved if everyone who joined the syndicate had to attend a meeting, have their signature witnessed in person and provide copies of their passport to verify their signature.

Over the next few days, I suggested that we should restrict the numbers of the syndicate by insisting that a live witnessed signature was required to join. Unfortunately, two of the ticket-holders were in Dubai and Portugal, and the original decision not to exclude anybody meant that the syndicate chose to rely on faxed signatures. This was much more risky – the person who received the cheque could simply deny the signature was his.

By Thursday, I had serious doubts about the whole idea. A small number of ticket-holders had not yet made contact, so I was in danger of joining a syndicate that had the worst possible number of members, plus only faxed forms for security. On Friday, at lunchtime, I received the forms prepared by the solicitor that Simon had engaged, and it dawned on me that I was jumping through hoops to do something I was not happy with. I felt I had a reasonable chance of picking the winner of the race, so I decided to go it alone. I now needed to make sure that I made my position absolutely clear to everyone involved. I phoned Simon and the solicitor to tell them my decision and faxed them written confirmation, sending hard copies by special delivery. The letter made it clear that I would not be part of the syndicate, and would not expect part of anyone else's winnings.

I took very little time to decide that Merry Masquerade had to be my selection. His recent form was terrific and it was hard to find any other horse on a fair weight whose form I liked.

On Saturday, Simon called to say that he had now heard from the remaining three ticket-holders and thought that he could get them all on board. He asked me to consider rejoining the group. A full group of 19 was a safe option, but I had rather warmed to the idea of relying on Merry Masquerade by then. There was also the problem of the letters I had sent, making it clear that I would have no claim over anyone's winnings, as it wasn't clear whether they could be legally revoked. I agreed to think it over on the way to Haydock.

With all called to mind, it seemed clear that I had to stick with my decision, and I told Simon this at the racecourse. The Tote had laid on a box for ticket-holders and the group went off for a hurried meeting to discuss strategy. The next time I saw Simon, his team had decided to play a bit of poker. He warned me that although they had 18 tickets for 18 runners, they were by no means forced to place one on each horse. He pointed out that they could leave out the outsiders and might place as many as four tickets on the favourite, so that I would only get 20 per cent of the pool if I did the same.

They were clearly keen to dissuade me from picking the favourite Merry Masquerade, and were hoping I'd chance my arm on another runner. However, I reckoned that if they were going to put four tickets on the favourite, then they would have chosen not to tell me, as it would then have suited them if I picked the same horse. I don't play a lot of poker but I can recognise a bluff when I see one. I was going for Merry Masquerade anyway. When push came to shove, the group placed two tickets on the favourite and one on all the others bar 100-1 outsider Treasure Chest.

It was some afternoon. Very few people had my new mobile number, so I had a pager that alerted me when a message had been left on my old number. In the next half-hour I received two alerts, which turned out to be angry messages, clearly from people not present, who were connected to the other ticket-holders. They seemed to have been under the impression that I had only left the syndicate on Saturday lunchtime, despite my efforts the previous day to make things absolutely clear in writing.

One said that I was dead if I picked the winner on my own. This left me a little shaken but, after what I had been through in the past couple of years, I was not going to be intimidated by that sort of nonsense.

Tim Watts was at Haydock, as he'd taken a share in my syndicate and was keen to enjoy the day. We stayed out of the Tote box and watched proceedings from a bar, and I was pleased when Merry Masquerade went off a heavily backed 15-8 favourite. He was usually held up, so I wasn't concerned when Andrew Thornton sat well off the pace. There was quite a bit of market strength behind Martin Pipe's contender Warner For Players, who had not run for two years. He made the running, and as they turned into the straight he was clearly the one to beat. Merry Masquerade made steady progress but in the testing conditions it was never going to be easy. Even when challenged and then headed, Warner For Players continued to battle on as my selection tired. As they made the long run for home from the final hurdle, I was desperately willing the winning line to arrive. Merry Masquerade just reached it first, a length and three-quarters ahead of Warner For Players.

Tim had been screaming our horse home from the second-last and now he erupted. He is as strong as an ox and he grabbed hold of me, lifted me off the ground and bounced me up and down while screaming "YES, YES, YES, YES". He then put me down and took to beating me on the back, Tarzan-style, while he continued his chant. After recovering from my beating, I headed to the winner's enclosure to make sure that no-one stole the jockey before he weighed in!

Some of the other ticket-holders congratulated me, some didn't. I knew that I'd gone out of my way to make my decision known to them so my conscience was clear. Unfortunately, a brilliant day at the races ended with another message on my pager – one of the earlier callers had returned with a sinister post-race threat. I put it to the back of my mind. A few other agents and a couple of my friends appeared for the evening celebration and we organised dinner for 12 in a private room at Reform, one of the top clubs in Manchester at the time.

There was plenty of coverage in the papers over the next few days, particularly in the *Racing Post*. There were one or two complaints from people who owned stakes in other tickets who still seemed not to be aware of the full facts. I wasn't in an easy position to defend myself, as it was the Post syndicate that had chosen a path different from that I would have recommended. Some of the Post coverage was more entertaining, as I was portrayed as having 'played hard and won big'. They explained that by refusing to rejoin the group on the Saturday, I pushed a guaranteed £80,000 in chips back into the middle and gambled it up to £512,000. After paying out my friends and agents, my share came to £312,958.95.

The Mail's headline compared my coolness to the Cincinnati Kid. A new magazine called Sports Adviser acclaimed me for the 'greatest put-away in recent punting history', theorising that I had concocted the syndicate plan from the start, always intending to withdraw. Mathematics clearly wasn't their strong point. It was in no-one's interest for there to be no syndicate at all, and it would have been foolish not to take part in the syndicate if a more suitable number, up to maybe 12, had joined.

And the messages on my pager? By chance, I was due to visit Cambridge police to tie up a loose end that dated back to my car being stolen by Hall. I mentioned the phone calls and they said they would look into it for me. When I got to the police station, I sat opposite the DC who had a list of telephone numbers that had called my phone. From my side of the desk, the list was unfortunately upside down. He pointed out that the police were not in the business of giving warnings and that if I wanted to take the matter further I would have to press criminal charges. Although the intent was clearly criminal, I decided that the people involved, perhaps unaware of the full facts, had made a mistake in the heat of the moment. I'd spare them a criminal prosecution on this occasion.

But, just for the record, I can read and memorise upside-down telephone numbers. The calls came from Ripon and central London. I'd say that there's one family that has a record of underestimating me.

CHAPTER 13

BIG WINS AND LOSSES, AND ANTE-POST BETTING

I CLASSIFY a really big touch as one that earns me in excess of £200,000 on a single race. If I include the Scoop6 bonus, I've done this five times. You will read about the Exponential coup – so who were the other three?

The Tony Carroll-trained Cerulean Rose, at Glorious Goodwood in 2003, sticks in the mind like toffee to a rug. I first spotted her a month earlier, when she showed great promise at Bath, and I was sufficiently impressed to back her next time at Lingfield, where she finished 14th of 16 after receiving what I would describe as an 'interesting' ride from Jamie Mackay. My interest had been pricked. I put my losses of £8,220 down to experience and expected to get them back before too long.

Next time out at Doncaster, almost a month later, Cerulean Rose again ran off a lowly handicap mark of 37. After Lingfield I wasn't certain what sort of ride to expect from little-known apprentice Liam Jones, but at 20-1 I was prepared to speculate a small amount and had £2,200 to win. Cerulean Rose received a much more aggressive ride this time and I was very happy with winnings of £44,000. I also considered backing her a week later at Chepstow, but had no reason to rate her better than the Doncaster form and so let her run unsupported. Oops. She won in such eye-catching style that I felt compelled to take a radical view of the performance. It suggested she was something to bet heavily on, especially if she was turned out again quickly while in such sparkling form.

The race at Chepstow took place on a very quiet Friday evening, which might well ensure that my knowledge of just how impressive she had been would not be widely shared within the betting industry. More importantly, it was only four days until the start of Glorious Goodwood. If Cerulean Rose were to turn out there in a five-furlong handicap, I would be able to go to war in an ultra-strong betting market.

As if by magic, Cerulean Rose was entered in a five-furlong handicap at Goodwood the following Wednesday. I wanted her as close as possible to the favoured far rail, so my cup was well on the way to running over when she was drawn highest of all in stall 23. It occurred to me that someone with more sympathy for the other side would have to feel guilty at being given such a huge opportunity. A horse I thought capable of winning with a stone more weight had been handed a gilt-edged chance thanks to the luck of the draw. That someone wasn't me.

Cerulean Rose was a typical punter's definition of the best bet I've ever had. She is the longest-priced horse ever that I considered almost sure to win. I would genuinely have been extremely surprised had she not done so. Cerulean Rose was the perfect dream bet for the man in the street. He could have walked into a betting shop and had a £1,000 bet accepted without question.

She was double smash material in spades, although I needed to be subtle with the first phase to avoid ruining the afternoon price. At early prices of around 6-1, I chose my opening salvos very carefully. As a result of this subterfuge, 6-1 was available on the opening show as well. Time for the heavy brigade. In a strong market the price fell to 9-2 at the off as I managed to get on £44,470.

There was a brief scare just after halfway when she was involved in a minor skirmish towards the far rail, but Cerulean Rose was soon in the clear and surged ahead to win by a smooth-looking length and a half. My profit of £262,027.50 was a personal record for a single bet. It would be three years before I bettered it.

Next up, the 2004 Wokingham Handicap at Royal Ascot. I've already referred to missing out on a monster touch on the unlucky Ellens Academy in 2001, but I more than made up for it three years later with Lafi.

Lafi was trained by David Nicholls. His reappearance run at Thirsk had caught my eye, to say the least, with his jockey Liam Treadwell not seeming at all keen to overexert himself. At Epsom next time, in finishing third, Lafi shaped like a horse about to strike form. As Nicholls' horses rarely peaked by their second outing of the season, I felt Lafi had a huge chance in the Wokingham. But there was a complication. The horse was part-owned by well-known tipster Henry Rix. If I waited until large amounts of money confirmed him an intended runner, I'd find the odds tumbling too quickly. On the other hand, if I steamed in too early and took all the best prices, the owners could quite rightly take exception and choose a different target, leaving me holding useless vouchers for Royal Ascot.

I had to wait and see. A few days later, Lafi shortened in price with three bookmakers. Someone was building a position. Time to build mine, although I'd have to make sure I placed the bets with enough subtlety to avoid upsetting anyone. Geoffrey Pooley and I organised just over £4,000 each-way, mostly at 16-1 with a bit of 20-1, of which my share came to £3,320 each-way. I didn't want too big a position in case the subsequent draw proved unfavourable. Luck was on my side again. Although this would level out in time, the draw was still of crucial importance at many meetings in 2004 and Royal Ascot was one of them.

Lafi had stall 30. Perfect. Word filtered through that the expected money from Rix and his cohorts had arrived on Friday lunchtime. I held my nerve, reckoning I'd wait until the Saturday, as if my team joined in too there was a danger of the price collapsing. I'd booked a suite at Pennyhill Park Hotel, not too far from Ascot, and had beaten the traffic the night before by taking the helicopter to the hotel helipad. Shortly before business opened on Saturday morning, I lined up my collection of mobile phones and summoned every agent I could locate.

The bad news was that Lafi was heavily tipped in that morning's *Racing Post*, which would make him very much more popular, but I was willing to take well under the top offer. Accordingly, I instructed my agents that the horse was a 'what you can get, 8 or bigger' situation. This meant that they were to place bets with no limit and take all the odds available of 10-1, 9-1 and 8-1.

My morning's business amounted to £14,363.70 each-way, but I hadn't finished. By the afternoon, Lafi's odds of 6-1 might have seemed very short for a race of this nature, but I felt that a £50,000 stake was appropriate and still believed the horse was overpriced. I organised a further £4,500 each-way at 6-1 and placed a £2,500 reverse forecast on Lafi and Dazzling Bay. Forecast betting pools are normally too small for me to bother with, but not in a race like this. All in, I'd staked £49,367.40.

Eddie Ahern sensibly kept Lafi closer to the pace than normal to avoid needing to switch wide. Horse and jockey then stormed through a furlong out to win by a length and a half. As I'd scooped £254,611.72, it was perhaps stretching a point and sympathy to consider myself unlucky – but if Dazzling Bay had managed to run one length closer and claim second instead of fifth, my winnings would have increased to almost £400,000.

It had been some week. The helicopter was taking me up to Yorkshire for a birthday party that evening and I had agreed to give a lift to Peter Easterby, who was in particularly fine form as his son

Tim's Fayr Jag had won the Group 1 Golden Jubilee Stakes that afternoon. Peter is a highly entertaining character, although his expert eye wasn't quite as sharp from the air. Towards the end of the flight, I put him on the satellite phone to his wife Marjorie, and he reported that he'd be back home ready for a cup of tea in ten minutes. Peter then looked out of the window and asked me which racecourse we were passing over. I was unable to resist teasing him for failing to recognise York, where he'd been a top trainer for decades.

The last horse in my big five is Silver Touch, who in September 2006 narrowly beat my record for a single horse with a win of £272,447.99. The figures for the top four singles are quite close to each other, which suggests that it is going to be hard for me to collect more than £300,000 in one hit. That won't stop me trying, though.

The most significant outcome of Silver Touch's success was that she was the one who took me over the £10 million mark since my troubles in Cambridge, sealing my decision to take the whole of 2007 off and enjoy a whole summer, as well as two winters, away from gambling. I still had the occasional punt, but didn't study racing over that period.

Once a trainer has made up his mind about a horse's trip, it can be hard to persuade him or her to reconsider. Silver Touch was trained by Mick Channon, and after her debut success over seven furlongs that April she ran twice over a mile. She was bred to stay that trip, but I was convinced she could excel at shorter distances and had to wait for Channon to 'come round to my way of thinking'!

Fortunately, he did, although it wasn't until early September that Silver Touch was entered in a seven-furlong Listed race at York. I couldn't see her being beaten and took further encouragement from the belief that the off-course betting market would be strong, with bookmakers taking the view that there are fewer secrets for them to worry about in races like this as opposed to lower-grade contests.

As before, it was a case of getting some decent bets on in the morning as subtly as possible to allow for a double smash, and Geoffrey and I managed to bury some large wagers in places that would not be too conspicuous. After morning prices of 9-2 and 4-1, Silver Touch did shorten up by the afternoon, as there seemed to be a big word for her at the track, so we had to take shorter prices on the opening show. With a carefully co-ordinated attack via the phones there were still plenty of places to get on, including the internet, betting shops and, finally, on this rare occasion, on-course. The York on-course market was very strong and as Silver Touch was clear second-favourite, the bookies were likely to be keen to lay some hefty bets. My father was racing that day with a couple of friends, so I arranged for £20,000 in cash to be at the track and travelled there to distribute it among the three of them, with strict instructions as to how it should be placed. I shan't name the other two, in case they are needed in future.

As Silver Touch entered the stalls, the final tally, including bets for my trading manager and a few others, was impressively long: £13,300 win, £8,300 place at 9-2, £23,000 win at 4-1, £1,000 each-way at 7-2, £14,900 win, £3,900 place at 100-30, £5,000 win at 3-1, £44,000 win at 11-4. It all added up to a whopping £101,200 win, £13,200 place, of which my share was £76,720 win and £10,560 place.

Given my past success, some in the betting industry will wonder how we managed stakes of this size, but it only happened by devoting hundreds of hours to devising the best possible system for the placing of bets. We needed to have different outlets available according to the type of race. In the case of Silver Touch, I am 99 per cent confident that not one of the bets struck was recognised as coming from a source connected to me. However, the biggest factor was the type of race. Placing large stakes on one of the market leaders in a Listed race is much easier than in races where the form is less well known. Bookmakers take much more field money in these races and are less wary of the contenders.

The result was never in doubt from halfway. A slow early pace was certain to suit Silver Touch and I could not see anything beating her for speed in the final two furlongs. Sure enough, she came through strongly to win fairly comfortably by a length and a quarter. Although my total winnings came to more than £272,000, it was the £56,000 cash profit from the betting ring that provided the most satisfaction. I stayed hidden behind the stands as my father and his two friends emerged with huge bundles of cash stuffed into every pocket. By the time we left the racecourse I looked like the Michelin Man.

We headed to the Marriott Hotel close to the racecourse. I'd stressed the need for total secrecy before and after the race, but in his excitement one of the group had forgotten his instructions. As we left the course, we bumped into journalist Tim Richards, who lives near York. When he asked how our day had gone, I swiftly interrupted the member of the group who had started to chuckle and reply "Well, yes . . ." My firm 'not too bad, probably about level' quickly reminded my one-off soldier of the rules. Back in my hotel room, we sent for champagne before getting down to counting the cash. It took some time, but no-one seemed to mind. Finally, I had to arrange for the money to be taken away securely for banking. I make a point of never keeping large amounts of cash at my house or on my person, being ever mindful of security.

The only other time I've had more than £50,000 on a horse was also a winner, albeit at much shorter odds, with Caesar Beware at Windsor in August 2004. We managed to get on £98,000, of which my share came to £77,680. The 11-10 favourite hosed up by six lengths and my winnings amounted to £95,416.

Now, let's turn to some losers. Although I don't back that many favourites, my biggest losses have tended to be on short-priced horses, simply because bigger stakes were possible. Five Years On, who never won a race in his life, set the record at Musselburgh in September 2004. He was expected to win very easily but finished fourth of six, and turned out to be one of those who gallop far better in the mornings than the afternoons. My losses came to £48,800.

I lost £39,800 on Always Waining at Goodwood in July 2004, and blew an almost identical amount when taking plenty of 11-10 about Strike Up The Band at Chester in May 2005. My other £40,000 reverse – which tends to be my 'normal' maximum, to all intents and purposes – was Quality Street at Sandown in July 2005.

It's rare that I go for a big bet ante-post. One substantial loser, however, was Three Valleys. After he won the Coventry Stakes at Royal Ascot in 2003 I had a monster bet on him for the following year's 2,000 Guineas. I thought he was the best two-year-old I had seen in some years and took all I could get each-way at 25-1, 20-1 and 16-1.

As seasoned ante-post players will know, late June is very early to have a serious view about a Classic race the following year. The horse was next due to run in the Group 1 Phoenix Stakes at the Curragh, and following reports of tremendous work at home I stepped in once more for the Guineas, taking another lump at around 12-1. The bet now stood to win me more than £300,000. However, after One Cool Cat and Old Deuteronomy had put him in his place – third – I stopped reckoning up the bookmakers' liabilities and turned to my own. They amounted to £26,400 when he beat only three horses home at Newmarket the following spring.

My most memorable ante-post winner was Love Divine in the 2000 Oaks. The market moved very quickly after her win in the Lupe Stakes at Goodwood and I had to take a variety of prices to achieve a decent position. I was very taken with her that day and was surprised when she wasn't made a warm favourite after the race. I stood to win just under £60,000 from my each-way stakes, but on the day I became increasingly convinced that she would win. I smashed into her that morning with win bets at 7-2, 3-1 and 11-4, topping up my stake to a total of £40,000.

I was so confident I decided to start the celebrations hours before the race. Pride goes before a fall – but not this time. The Robot was sent to HMV and came back with a suitably chosen CD of hymns – very much a first for my CD collection, but I recalled that 'Love Divine' was a hymn we'd been forced to sing at school. Over lunch, the CD was set up as the voicemail message on all my mobile phones.

Love Divine was given a sound tactical ride by Richard Quinn and won comfortably without providing a moment's anxiety, thereby ensuring winnings of £142,065.64. The phone calls flooded in from my agents after the race, but I took the rest of the afternoon off and headed for the gym. As I didn't answer any of my phones, everyone who called was greeted by a bunch of boy sopranos blaring out "Love Di-i-vine all loves excelling".

Media Puzzle in the 2002 Melbourne Cup was another great antepost touch. I'd received a good word for the horse a few weeks before the race and got some decent bets on at 33-1 and 25-1. As it was the end of the turf season, I indulged myself and tinkered with how the bet was shared, so that I stood to win exactly £100,000.

Staying cool and collected as a gambler is as important a technique as any part of the selection process. I think this race illustrated better than any other how I had come very close to mastering this elusive art. The Cup was due off at 4.10am UK time, so I set my alarm for 4.09am. I had a big night out planned the following evening, so I wanted to get back to sleep as quickly as possible. Five minutes later, Media Puzzle had won smoothly by a couple of lengths. Two minutes after that, I was asleep. I can imagine many punters being critical. Surely, I can hear them say, why not enjoy the moment? But waking up the next morning and remembering that you won £100,000 during the night – that's enjoying the moment.

Surprisingly, my biggest ante-post win came over jumps with Rooster Booster in the 2003 Champion Hurdle. It had been years since I'd been a serious student of jump form, but a call from one of my sources at the beginning of November alerted me to his prospects. Bets were struck at 25-1 and 20-1, and a second wave of business a couple of weeks later saw me step in for a large top-up, mostly at 10-1. In the Champion Hurdle, he slaughtered the opposition by 11 lengths. I'd decided that as it was a jump race and outside the Flat season, I'd waive my 'no cheering' rule and shout him home with two of my agents who had also backed him. In a rare outbreak of ill-discipline I was far noisier than you'd ever see me when I back a winner on the Flat. Winning £154,500 on a jump race was a great way to start the Flat season the following week.

CHAPTER 14

SIX-FIGURE TOUCHES AND RECORD WEEKS

SIX-FIGURE wins have been reasonably common over the years, most based on the form book and nearly all of those in handicaps. In May 2002, I had a monster day during the York Dante meeting. Five bets, four winners. Showpiece and White Cliffs won at Salisbury and Imtiyaz prevailed at York, but the biggest winner was Macaw at York. I wasn't massively confident, but the opening show of 33-1 was too big and my each-way bets were to win me £111,045. However, as I watched the race from the owners' bar, I found myself next to a group of Scotsmen who were cheering him home pretty much from the moment the stalls opened. It was clear from their support that he'd been especially prepared for the race and I only wished I'd known. I'd have taken all prices down from 33-1 if I'd been aware of the confidence behind him.

Master Robbie was a big-priced touch at Ascot in September 2003. My team returned me a total of £2,435 each-way at 50-1 and 40-1 and his victory led to a profit of £126,010. When he won at 20-1, some reports suggested that the big-priced winner was sure to be a good result for the bookmakers. This wasn't the case.

Salviati was another major result on a sunny Sunday at Newbury in August 2004. He hadn't won for more than a year but was an out-standing form pick in a sprint handicap. We found some nice quiet accounts to place my bet of £25,000, mainly at 9-2, clearing £113,176. Four days later, I took everything available at 5-2, 9-4 and 2-1 about Morgan Lewis at Haydock, turning a stake of £49,410 into a profit of

£114,188. On his previous start he had been so unlucky that I actually noted down 'very easy winner' in my notes, underlined twice. Three days later came my Caesar Beware bet. I was in true 'thunderstorm' form, a term I use for a period of weeks when I hit a rich vein of form and turn over huge sums each week to capitalise on this.

Sea Frolic, in June 2005, left me mystified as to how I'd won £126,687.50 at a minor evening meeting at Warwick. Happily mystified, but bemused nonetheless. The takings were around twice what I had expected, and there were two reasons. Firstly, Royal Ascot started the next day and the bookmakers were probably fielding much higher turnover than usual. Secondly, the race was once again the type to reassure the bookmakers, a 15-runner handicap. Even with these three factors, I still felt we had the luck of the draw that night. Getting just short of £10,000 each-way on a horse backed from 12-1 to 9-1 on a Monday evening was an amazing result. It felt even better when Sea Frolic played her part in proceedings by crossing the line a length and a half in front.

That was the start of a magical seven days in which I set a new record for a week's trading. My previous two record weeks had been achieved in successive years at Glorious Goodwood. Some have suggested that Goodwood is a terrible place for betting, but with lifetime profits of more than a million pounds there I have no hesitation in nominating it as far and away my favourite track.

The reason I like it, and perhaps others don't, is that races are more complicated to assess than at most tracks. The eccentric switchback nature of the course means that certain horses handle it far better than others. This might seem like a negative point but if I'm seeking a big edge over the bookmakers, this is most likely to happen in races that are as difficult as possible. Crucially, I find it relatively simple to forecast the way in which the race will be run. Cerulean Rose was a much bigger price than she would have been in a similar race at another track, because the layers were bamboozled by the general belief that handicaps at Goodwood are fiendishly complicated puzzles.

My profit in Goodwood week 2003 was £436,012.24, with Cerulean Rose supported by profits of £91,250 on Lady Bear in the mile handicap and £96,894 from Patavellian in the Stewards' Cup. In 2004, my profit was £413,012.24. Salviati at Newbury, as mentioned above, was the biggest winner that week but I found a whole barrage of smaller winners at Goodwood, including £69,500 from Merlin's Dancer. One day from that week is outlined in much greater detail in part three.

But, returning to 2005, Royal Ascot week at York would see me better those figures. Technically, Acomb doesn't qualify as a six-figure winner, but two wins of more than £80,000 in the space of five days makes it very hard to leave him out. I hadn't backed Acomb on the first of three quick wins, on the same night as Sea Frolic, but the way he won convinced me that he was very well treated. When he reappeared at Ayr five days later I was ready to open my shoulders for a serious punt. It was still Royal York week and the bookmakers were still trading more heavily, even on the smaller meetings. My bet of £15,000 at 6-1 and 11-2 was fairly easily placed by my trading manager and Acomb made all the running to give me a profit of £85,140.

Iffraaj, in the Wokingham Handicap on the Saturday, was the other big winner of the week. Because of the switch to York the Wokingham had a much smaller field, 17 runners instead of 30, and Iffraaj stood out like an apple in a bowl of cherries. When the weights were published I had to move fast to secure double-figure prices, but Iffraaj was very popular and my bets weren't fully accommodated. A week or two later I had to be brave and get stuck in again at 6-1. There was always the concern that I might get blown off course by a big draw bias, but I couldn't afford to wait and watch the price contract day by day. The decision proved correct, as Iffraaj was such a heavily backed favourite that he started at the unthinkably short price for a Wokingham of 9-4. He sped home two lengths in front and my winnings came to £119,980.

The best of the other winners that week, both on Friday, were Munsef winning me £70,728.86 in the King George V Handicap and La Chunga £50,582.84 in the Albany Stakes. My overall profit on the week of £455,471.53 was a new record. Just as well, as a little more than a month later I suffered my worst losing week. I've already referred to the £40,000 loss on Quality Street, but having won more than a million pounds in the previous ten weeks I was in 'thunderstorm' mode, and my losses of £146,725.71 were a weekly record. Given the circumstances, it wasn't an irretrievable situation. When a longer losing run hits it is hard to remain so relaxed, and it becomes impossible to avoid a certain amount of mental torment.

Back to Acomb. It is quite rare for me to follow up on a horse I have previously backed on a form basis, but in his case I felt that neither of his wins in York week had shown him to best advantage. At Epsom, just four days after Ayr, I felt he had an outstanding chance to win again and, to my amazement, the market seemed keen to oppose him. It's great when that happens. We got most of our bet on at 4-1 and I upped my stake to £20,000, winning £82,290 as Acomb made all once again.

A month later, Roodeye was another to net me a big touch at an evening meeting at Doncaster. We had found one particular outlet willing to lay us massive bets, and for the short time it lasted we took full advantage. A large part of my £13,000 each-way was placed with a single account and offers of around 8-1 were seriously misguided. The profit came to £124,360.

Finally, back to where we came in – the Scoop6. After my triumph in 2000, there were two further big incidents. I've played the Scoop6 less than a dozen times since then, as I prefer to wait for large rollovers and a card I fancy before becoming involved. July 22, 2000 was one such occasion when a £1m rollover in the win fund was up for grabs. There was massive demand, and I needed a good result or two to knock out the other players. This came up in spades in the third race. I'd become steadily convinced that the quality of form in Germany was improving, so I'd included the 20-1 German-trained Abitara in my selections. Her victory dramatically reduced the number of surviving tickets and left me with serious prospects of scooping the lot.

But, just as I began to see a huge pot heading my way, it suddenly slipped from my grasp. I'm fairly sure that I had all but one of the remaining tickets on Blue Sugar, who surged clear a furlong out in the fifth leg. I also had all the runners covered in the last leg, so was incredibly well placed to scoop the million on my own. But disaster struck. Blue Sugar started to tire in the closing few yards and was collared on the line by Jathaabeh. It was a bitter blow.

In May 2004, I again came within a whisker of collecting half a million when chasing the Scoop6 bonus rollover. Once again, I had included my agents, but this time the winnings in the first week were more substantial. I'd had two winning tickets in the win fund, yielding a profit of £189,500, of which my share was £115,938.58.

There were four winning tickets chasing a bonus rollover of just over £1m the following week. The case for us all forming a syndicate was overwhelming, and news soon filtered through that another professional punter, Harry Findlay, had the other tickets. Harry, part-owner of star chaser Denman, is an enormous and successful player, although he tends to favour a riskier strategy with his capital than I do.

Come the following Saturday, Harry and I picked out four selections in the race at Newbury. I still can't believe we didn't collect. Not only did we choose Cold Turkey, who was beaten a short head by the Ed Dunlop-trained Swift Tango (I think I mentioned earlier that

I wasn't a big Dunlop fan, well, here's one of the reasons), but we also selected Red Fort, who finished third, and Wunderwood, both of whom went on to win at Royal Ascot next time out. Half a million pounds went astray by a short head. Still, you don't go into the gambling business without expecting a few minor disappointments . . .

CHAPTER 15

PROFESSIONAL OWNER

FROM the age of 15, from the moment the betting shop door swung open, I had little doubt that I wanted to make a living from backing horses. At the time it seemed a fantastic way to earn serious money and I still wouldn't swap it for anything. However, as time went by, the intensive nature of some of the work became a little monotonous, and becoming a racehorse owner has definitely spiced up my workload.

I'm proud that I've achieved something almost unique in long-term racehorse ownership – I've made a substantial profit. The average racehorse owner in the UK suffers a loss of more than 70p in the pound on his investment, so I've needed a combination of detailed research into potential purchases, careful choice of trainers and successful punting to achieve a return. The profit isn't nearly as high per hour worked as from my day-to-day gambling, but the thrill of owning winners, including successes at most of the top meetings, has more than made up for that. I've owned the winners of more than 130 races and enjoyed every minute of it.

For simplicity, I'll refer to the horses as mine, although in most cases I've been the majority stakeholder alongside smaller shareholders, often agents or friends. Owners are allowed to register their horses as partnerships, and can choose a partnership name that allows the identity of the partners to be confidential, although the names are submitted to racing's rulers, the BHA. It has been suggested that all owners' names should be fully declared to the public, but I don't agree. Providing they are correctly registered with the authorities, I don't feel it is in racing's interests to discourage ownership by people who prefer their affairs to be confidential.

When I bought Pevensey in the autumn of 2006, I devoted a huge amount of time to picking him from the 2,000 or so horses for sale at that time. That time spent was rewarded when he won at Royal Ascot the following year. He opened at 16-1 that day, a price that would surely not have been available had the bookmakers been gifted the information that he was my choice from all those horses the previous year. I make no apology for the fact that I have, on most occasions, kept information about horses I own out of the public domain. That hasn't stopped the bookmakers endlessly speculating but, from what I've heard, they are wrong so often that I sometimes feel embarrassed for them. If they want to spend their time chasing such information I'll be happy to organise some wild goose chases for them.

Buying horses is never easy, although I've been helped in my shopping by the flexibility of not needing to have a set number in training or a specific type, so I am able to focus on just finding the best value I can. Apart from the breeze-up sales, I rely on my own assessments of the form of a horse, or of its relatives if it has never raced. I only frequent British sales, although I did make one trip to Goffs in Ireland searching for yearlings with a couple of helpers. We returned empty-handed after I formed the impression that, on their own turf, the Irish vendors were perhaps a little too clever for me.

After some success with Pertemps FC in my comeback year, I bought Minivet after he finished second in a York claimer in October 1999. He had very sound form on the Flat, was rated 87, and it was a bit of a surprise that his owners let him take his chance in a claimer for the modest price of £22,000. Perhaps it was because he had a club foot, a defect that would put off many paddock judges. He made his jumps debut for me in a two-mile novice hurdle at Wetherby the next month, a race that turned out to be a little controversial. Tim Easterby reported that Minivet had schooled well and might be worth a small interest, but in the race jockey Lorcan Wyer gave the leaders a very large head start before finishing strongly in the closing stages. Having seen Minivet drift markedly in the betting, I was less than happy, but kept my own counsel.

I had a decent bet next time at Doncaster, when Minivet won a novice hurdle easily. He went from strength to strength that winter, winning four more times at Kelso, Musselburgh, Doncaster again and Ayr. I was enthralled by my new venture.

At the end of the year, I decided to try a number of new trainers, and William Haggas was one of those at the top of my list. William had earned a reputation for shrewdness and I had no hesitation in choosing him to train Great News, a four-year-old gelding I bought for £40,000 at the Newmarket sales. As usual, I pointed out that betting was a key concern in my ownership but that giving illicit instructions to jockeys wouldn't be on the agenda. The trainer's job was to tell me as accurately as possible when my horse was at the peak of his form. Together we would carefully choose our entries and, once a horse came into peak form, we'd fix a target.

Great News didn't please William at all in the spring of 2000. He just didn't show any sparkle. One of our decisions had been not to leave horses at home in their boxes if they were healthy. Most horses would recapture their form in due course if they were sound and genuine and, in the meantime, they would drop down the handicap if they weren't winning. After three runs at a mile and three more at a mile and a quarter Great News had still not returned to form, but the races hadn't been wasted as he'd been dropped 16lb to an attractive mark of 67. William felt that Great News was turning the corner and suggested we take a break to see if he could freshen the horse up to bring him back to somewhere near his best. It turned out to be worth the wait.

It was late August before William was sufficiently upbeat about Great News, and he felt there were suitable handicaps over both seven furlongs and a mile at the Ayr Western meeting in the middle of September. It's the biggest Flat meeting of the year in Scotland, renowned for strong betting markets as well as plenty of after-hours entertainment. We picked out the seven-furlong handicap on the Friday.

In his final gallop, Great News finished alongside Courting, who won a Listed race at Yarmouth at long odds three days before Ayr. Gallops can be misleading but the signs were encouraging. I wanted to have a serious bet, as I didn't see how Great News could be beaten if he was indeed back to form. Although afternoon betting markets are invariably much stronger, I wanted to get cracking in the morning. I wanted a double smash.

Friday's *Racing Post* brought disappointing news on the Great News front. They had installed him as 7-2 favourite, although at least they had tipped against him. However, I guessed that Ladbrokes would have a big influence on the shaping of the market, as I'd noticed they often took a view about the Haggas horses. By then, I had a fairly good idea about the identity of the mole in the yard who might be betting with them. I discussed it with William as a matter of urgency and we were careful to take measures lest news of the gallop reached Ladbrokes and ruined the planned coup. Lo and behold, when the early prices came out, Ladbrokes had indeed taken a view and were top price of 11-2 about Great News, compared to the 9-2 available elsewhere. It seemed that their line of communication had suffered a temporary breakdown.

I took advantage by sending a wave of business across the industry, taking all prices from 11-2 down to 7-2. Ladbrokes seemed fairly convinced of their position and were still offering the biggest price at lunchtime. There were further heavy investments at 7-2 and 3-1 on the opening show, and the double smash was complete with an SP of 11-4. The race itself was less worrying than the preamble, with Great News always going smoothly and winning by a length and a quarter. I had won £126,526 from a stake of just under £30,000 – not a colossal sum for a double smash, but very satisfying considering the disappointing forecast price.

That was not the end of the week's business. Great News was in the Ayrshire Handicap the following day – sponsored by Ladbrokes, no less – and that provided a further opportunity to relieve the sponsors and their competitors of some more money. Despite the step up in grade Great News opened a much shorter price the next day and, backed from 11-4 to 2-1, again won comfortably, this time netting me £43,463. Still basking in the memory of Grangeville landing a big gamble at the same meeting 12 months earlier, I drove home with two large trophies on the back seat of the car. I was certainly keen to return.

Dim Sums was another to hit the jackpot for me that year. I homed in on him after his victory in a nursery at Pontefract in July on his third start. He won off a mark of 79, far from the rating of a top horse, but I was really impressed by the way he won in a very fast time. I felt he could step up in grade and bought him privately from trainer David Barron.

Dim Sums ran his first race for me at Newmarket three weeks later. It was Frankie Dettori's first day back in the saddle after his light aeroplane crashed at the course two months earlier, killing pilot Patrick Mackey. He was full of fun when he saw me in the paddock. We had met only once before, on a water-skiing boat in Dubai four years earlier, but he walked straight up to me and asked 'Eh Pat, this your 'orse?' I talked him through my views on the draw – a lot more politely than I had with Kevin Darley at Newcastle the year before – as we were drawn in the middle, six of 12, and I wanted to race closer to the stands' rail, where the fastest ground was.

I didn't have a large bet as the race was a huge step up in grade. Frankie's first ride back, Atlantis Prince, had been a hugely popular winner, and his fans were playing up their winnings on Dim Sums, his only other ride of the day. Dim Sums was quite headstrong coming out of the stalls, but he soon relaxed and sped home by a length and a half.

He gave us a bigger payday next time out when winning the £93,000 Redcar Two-Year-Old Trophy, going off a warm 6-4 favourite and never looking in much danger of defeat. The race provided us with a handy selling opportunity, as I had doubts as to how much Dim Sums would improve over the winter. Two big offers came in over the next ten days, one from Sheikh Mohammed's agent John Ferguson – sadly not one of his multi-million-pound bids – and a slightly higher offer from America. We took the dollars and Dim Sums was away across the Atlantic for a tidy profit. It turned out to be the perfect time to sell, as he never recaptured his form.

All through that season, David's mastery of the training of Dim Sums shone though. After his victory at Newmarket there had been time for two or three other runs before Redcar, but David felt that Dim Sums was not quite right and insisted he stayed at home. He brought him back to his peak for October, which is no mean feat when a horse has been on the go since March.

One attempted coup that went astray that year was an each-way gamble on Mary Jane, trained by Nigel Tinkler. Backed from 33-1 to 11-2, she was beaten only a couple of lengths but just lost out on the place money – and even fourth place would have netted a profit of around £50,000. Then there was the unreliable Threat, who failed to land a gamble at Haydock. Backed from 16-1 to 6-1, he missed out on a place by half a length. A week later, he was one of the market leaders in a competitive handicap at the Doncaster St Leger meeting and managed to win, but I had lost confidence in his attitude and wasn't willing to invest on him at a top meeting.

Mr Pertemps, trained by Stuart Williams, was another near miss in 2000 when runner-up at Hamilton, backed from 10-1 to 3-1. We were disappointed with the price, though, as the horse had been backed at 25-1 in very light morning trading. Although I've suffered comparatively few leaks over the years, it can be very frustrating when it happens and I've been unable to identify the source. In this case, detection proved easy. Gavin Faulkner was Stuart's stable jockey at the time, and although he was not riding at Hamilton he asked Stuart a few days after the race whether he could expect a present from the each-way bets, as the horse had been 25-1 in the morning. The morning price had not been reported anywhere and Faulkner rather gave the game away about his part in the leak.

However, the year ended on a high note when Inzacure, trained by Ralph Beckett, landed a gamble from 25-1 to 9-1 at Brighton. Inzacure was owned by Major Pooley and a few of his chums, although if I think really hard I can recall being involved in the betting action that day.

The Great News story was not so profitable in 2001. Held back by one or two problems, he had run only twice by September. Although he was not as well handicapped as before, we still had in mind another crack at the Ladbrokes Ayrshire Handicap. However, he didn't work nearly so well in the run-up to that race and William told me that he would need a run to put him right.

At Ayr, Great News was forecast to be one of the market leaders, yet William didn't really fancy him. Marnor, on the other hand, trained by Mick Easterby, was seriously fancied. He had tumbled down the ratings since joining Easterby and had run with promise a week earlier at Doncaster. I had quite a hefty bet on him and, needless to say, nothing on Great News. It was a perfect example of how horses can make fools of us all. Great News was never far away and stole the initiative over Marnor at a crucial stage, in the end holding on by three-quarters of a length. There was my horse, in the winner's enclosure, and there was the one I'd had a decent bet on, standing next to him in the runner-up's spot. Ah, life's little ironies. I didn't blame William, of course, as racing is far from an exact science and he had been spot-on about Great News throughout the previous two years.

I'd already had a much better day that month when Prince Cyrano, a £30,000 purchase, landed the Doncaster breeze-up sales race, held at Kempton, by five lengths. I missed the race, as I was keeping my mother company while my father underwent a triple heart bypass operation. It was an incredibly stressful period, but news of Prince Cyrano's win was a welcome distraction and half an hour later the hospital called to report that everything had gone smoothly. Suddenly, we had two major causes for celebration. I'd asked Private Brearley to take the trophy straight to my parents' house, as I planned to take it along when we visited my father in hospital the next day. Then word filtered back that the trophy from a £50,000 race was a tiny silver ashtray. Stand easy, Private Brearley.

Next stop for Prince Cyrano was Chantilly, for the Group 3 Prix d'Arenberg three days later, as Stuart felt he was the type to recover quickly and the race looked an average affair for a Group contest. We thought we'd found the perfect opportunity for some winning black type, but the local hope Dobby Road ran him out of it by a short neck. At this point I was keen to sell Prince Cyrano. The races at Chantilly and Kempton had not been strong and on pedigree I wasn't convinced he would progress.

In a bid to enhance Prince Cyrano's sale value, we threw him in at the deep end against his elders and betters in the Group 1 Prix de l'Abbaye. To be truthful, he had no chance whatsoever, but I hoped that if he raced on the quickest part of the track he might perform with sufficient credit to increase the prospects of a profitable sale. Sure enough, his finishing position of ninth of 19 in the top sprint of the late season added a few pounds to his price-tag, and he went on to make £120,000 at Newmarket sales that month.

CHAPTER 16
THE VELCRO PHONES

HAVING started out with Tim Easterby in 1999, I'd now got to know his uncle, Mick Easterby. Mick and his brother Peter, Tim's father, have been legendary trainers in Yorkshire for decades, shrewdness personified, and are also renowned for the large chunks of North Yorkshire they now own on the back of it. Peter had passed on the reins to Tim in the late 1990s but Mick is still going strong, assisted by his son David.

Mick has a reputation for canny deals and an equal reputation for needing careful handling, as he's very keen on getting his own way. Earlier in 2001, he told me that he thought he might land a touch with Itsanothergirl and persuaded me to lease her, as the owner had fallen on hard times. Itsanothergirl had been out of form in the spring but Mick had kept her busy and the handicapper had dropped her quickly to 50 from a rating of 70. Neither the handicapper nor betting public were wary of her, because it was clear from watching her races that the jockeys had been out there having a go every time she ran.

After a summer break to freshen her up, Itsanothergirl was ready to find a little handicap, and a race on an August Saturday evening at Haydock was chosen. That day I'd need the 'Velcro phones' with me. Operating at the racecourse required a large number of phones if a major bet was planned. Rather than carrying a briefcase full of loose phones, I had my office staff make up a clipboard with Velcro all over it. The other side of the Velcro was then stuck on the back of the phones, and this allowed 14 phones to stick firmly to one A4-sized clipboard. With papers placed on top it wouldn't arouse any interest, as it would just look like a large pile of documents until I sprang into action.

Itsanothergirl was totally unconsidered at 20-1 on the first show, but once my troops went to war she was backed at all rates down to 5-1. The weather that evening was atrocious, with some of the wettest conditions I'd experienced at the races, but heavy ground was ideal for the mare. We felt that ten and a half furlongs was probably a maximum for her, so Mick made sure that jockey Philip Robinson would be patient with her in the first part of the race. Robinson carried out his instructions perfectly, bided his time and then produced Itsanothergirl to take the lead in the final furlong and go on to win by a length and a quarter.

The Velcro phones were busy before the race, but it was only my main mobile that was hectic afterwards as Mick was in terrific form, treating me to a full rundown of his mastery of the training profession. Mick is certainly keen to leave no-one in any doubt as to his talents. His brother Peter has plenty of stories too, but they tend to be more about other characters in racing. Only once, after a couple of drinks, have I heard him talk in detail about his Gold Cup and Champion Hurdle winners. Mick, on the other hand, will talk to you all day about his big-race successes, including with 1,000 Guineas winner Mrs McArdy and July Cup winner Lochnager.

Lectures from Mick are also compulsory on a wide range of other racing topics, including the handling of all equine problems. Indicating to him that a subject has been covered before doesn't have any effect in shortening the lecture. For example, when breathing problems are mentioned, replying with 'You're a master of them, aren't you?' gets a firm reply of 'I am that' followed by the detailed explanation.

Inevitably, there have been one or two difficulties in dealing with such a colourful character. Mick approved of my total discretion with any information I received, but couldn't understand why I wasn't able to be indiscreet with what I had heard from other stables. He nicknamed me The Gleaner, claiming that I was much better at gleaning things than revealing them. He said he would name a horse after me, which I didn't take seriously until The Gleaner, now a winner over fences, made its debut a few years ago.

Mick is at his most entertaining when a microphone is thrust under his nose in the winner's enclosure, and got into hot water a few years ago when he used a four-letter word rhyming with 'hunt' on Channel 4 Racing. Afterwards, although hardly full of remorse, Mick was full of ideas for sorting out his mistake. At first he tried suggesting that the word had a different meaning in Yorkshire. When that ploy failed, his son David received a call hinting that he should go on TV to imply that his father was senile. "Tell them I've gone over t'top", his dad suggested.

David and I have become firm friends. He has already proved himself a champion trainer in the point-to-point field and will no doubt do very well when he takes over from his father. That may take some while, however, as Mick is not one to cede power lightly. Mick and I had a minor falling out a couple of years ago after I did a deal to send a couple of horses to him, only for Mick to insist on changing the deal after they had arrived. Things didn't work out and I had to fax the trainer to point out that he had moved the goalposts. Normal relations have now been restored, but Mick obviously liked my turn of phrase because, with his finely tuned ability for writing his own version of history, he now tells people with a glint in his eye: "That Patrick's all right, but you have to watch 'im, he tried to move t'goalposts on a deal with me a couple of years back."

Moving a few miles north-west, I bought Downland in 2000 and sent him to David Barron. The stable is as reliable as they come for churning out a healthy stream of winners every year, so a long spell out of form in 2001 was most unusual. By the time September rolled around, however, David thought he had his string back in form and felt that Downland was ready to win a handicap at Haydock.

The horse looked particularly well handicapped to me and I stepped in for a major punt at morning and afternoon show odds, double smashing the price from 14-1 to 11-2. However, disaster struck when Downland got loose on the way to the start and wasted valuable energy before the race began. This almost invariably leads to defeat and so it proved here, with David's last-minute calls to the track to withdraw the horse not arriving in time. Downland finished eighth of 15 and I had done my money in cold blood.

In the expectation of him winning that day, we had made an advance entry for Downland in a major handicap at Ascot. We put that out of our minds after Haydock, convinced that he had not run well enough even allowing for the mishap. But on the Monday before Ascot, the day entries were confirmed, I noticed that the ground seemed likely to be soft and, with Downland set to carry a very low weight, I rang David and suggested we should give it a go. On the morning of the race, Downland was as big as 66-1 in the morning betting. There was no danger of my having a huge bet in a much stronger race, particularly as David's stable was still not fully firing, but I couldn't resist having an each-way bet at those odds despite the rise in grade.

I had been seeing the racing presenter Emma Ramsden, now married to jockey Jamie Spencer, in a somewhat fiery on-off relationship for most of 2001. She was quite an astute judge of form and, amused by my bets on Downland, correctly pointed out that he had no chance on any recent form and accused me of having a sentimental punt simply because I owned him. This followed on from the evening before when, after a serious losing week, she had suggested that I should change my title from Field Marshal to Failed Marshal.

Just after the two-furlong pole, a horse loomed up travelling ominously easily on the stands' side. Emma asked: "What's the one in light blue?" As calmly as I could, I drawled: "That . . . would be Downland." He swept home unchallenged, winning me £159,565.55. I certainly hadn't been confident or I'd have had bigger bets and the SP would not have been 40-1. The profit from Downland's victory went down particularly well, recouping my losses from my week as the Failed Marshal.

Funnily enough, I was in a nightclub in a racing town a few months later where a few jockeys were partying. On hearing that I was an owner, David Kinsella, a lightweight rider who barely tips the scales at seven stone, came up to me, drew himself up to his full 5' 2" and inquired why I hadn't recognised his talents and given him any opportunities. I asked him what his biggest winner as a jockey had been. "Downland, September 29 at Ascot," he answered. "So who owned that then?" I replied with a smile. Jockeys don't all have the best of memories, you know.

The 'Velcro phones' were back in action at the end of October when I attended Tattersalls sales in Newmarket. Quantica was running for me in a nursery at Redcar and trainer Nigel Tinkler and I both felt he was ready to win, but we were both busy at the sales. The sales complex at Newmarket is a little bit public for organising a gamble, but we found a small annexe room that had some comfortable chairs and was quiet. We hurriedly moved in and switched the television over to the Redcar coverage. The only other person in there, English-born American trainer Simon Bray, didn't mind the rapid change in programming, but a surprised expression stole across his face when I produced enough phones to run a small call centre and started using them in feverish fashion. The betting show came through quite late from Redcar so I was still receiving calls halfway through the race – which Quantica won by a couple of lengths at 10-1, having opened at 14-1.

It was a busy day at the sales, so as soon as we knew the result Nigel and I stood up, shook hands, and without saying a word grabbed our things and went back out to the sale. Gambling with bookmakers is illegal in most US states so I don't think Simon had ever seen anything like it. The look of amazement on his face was a picture. With a profit of £128,587, that little room at Tattersalls became known as the 'coup room'.

A plan that failed to come off involved Three Days In May, the horse I bought and named after my epiphany at the Curragh and the bonanza betting period that followed. She landed a gamble for me at Thirsk in 2002 but didn't really progress, so I just wanted to win another little race with her before selling her at the end of the season. She looked to have a squeak in a moderate six-furlong handicap at Lingfield, and William Haggas and I felt that as she had nothing in hand with the handicapper, it was worth using an apprentice jockey whose allowance would reduce the weight she had to carry. I suggested Natalia Gemelova, who was based with Nigel Tinkler. Natalia wasn't the strongest apprentice in the weighing room but she could claim the full 7lb allowance. Her name on the racecard also had the bonus of being highly likely to increase the starting price of Three Days In May, as bookmakers would reason that a high-powered Newmarket trainer like William Haggas was unlikely to book a girl apprentice for a fancied runner. Three Days In May went off at 20-1.

I was convinced from recent evidence that the quickest ground that day would be on the far side. Conventional wisdom indicated that the far side was only the place to be when the ground was soft, but conventional wisdom won't get you far in this business and I believed that my analysis of recent results was correct. Our draw in stall one of 20 would also help.

The plan worked a treat for three of the six furlongs. At halfway Natalia was making her way home in splendid isolation on the far side, but we all know what happens to the best-laid plans, and this one went the same way. Three Days In May ran a fine race but found one too good in the 16-1 shot Seel Of Approval, who won by a length and a half from stall 4 (at least I was right about the low numbers). Seel Of Approval won again next time out and picked up four races the following season, whereas Three Days In May never won again. With the benefit of hindsight, Seel Of Approval was an absolute certainty that day. It was only the large advantage of the far-side ground that allowed us to get so close to him.

Curfew was another horse to give me great pleasure, not least because she was one of a handful to race in my name and colours. I'd bought her after a stunning performance at the breeze-ups and she was sent to be trained by James Fanshawe. After she'd won first time out as a two-year-old, I decided to use my own dark blue and beige colours as we were hoping to campaign her in a higher grade. When I rang James to ask how she was progressing, he said: "Put it this way, I'd like to find one who can go past her." He thought she was his best two-year-old and word from sources in Newmarket suggested that most in the yard felt the same. I had a nice bet on her at 7-2 when she won on her debut at Yarmouth in a seven-furlong maiden, and in the late summer of 2003 she picked up three seven-furlong handicaps within three weeks, culminating in a quite valuable contest at Salisbury.

New Year's Eve in 2002 saw me tucked up in bed early, as soon as I'd seen the new year in, as I knew I had business to do the following day. Mr Pertemps had been moved from Stuart Williams to Richard Fahey, as Stuart reckoned he had become bored by Newmarket and would benefit from a change of scenery. After a couple of months, Richard reported that he had freshened up Mr Pertemps and he was working well at home. With a handicap rating of only 38, he was well worth backing next time he appeared.

With a horse rated so low, there were very few opportunities, but we found a small race on New Year's Day at Southwell. It seemed certain that Mr Pertemps would open up at a big price as he had been totally out of form when last seen in the summer. As Richard's stable was increasing in size, I felt it best to take a price in the morning, despite the weak market, just in case there was a leak. I hoped that the New Year's Day market might react more slowly than normal as bookmakers struggled with their hangovers.

I was up very early with a clear head and, with internet coverage not as wide as it is today, I was soon hunting around central London for a newsagent that was open. Most people on the street at that time were straggling home after a very big night and morning, I think I was the only one walking straight. I eventually found one on Oxford Street and returned to the office. Most of my soldiers were dragged out of bed by 9.30am and were set to move in at 10am. Mr Pertemps duly opened up at 20-1 with quite a few firms and we took all that was available at double-figure prices. That afternoon, Channel 4 were covering racing from Cheltenham, but they drew plenty of attention to the gamble that had taken place at Southwell. They even showed the race, despite not planning any coverage from the track, and their viewers were treated to the sight of Mr Pertemps strolling home by three lengths, proving in the process that he was much better than a 38-rated horse. The attention was entertaining, although not ideal in terms of keeping my horses low-profile, and certainly got the new year off to a flying start.

After further successes, I later left Richard's yard following a lengthy bad run during which horses failed to perform as expected. One of the horses concerned was Mr Lear, who won twice in succession over hurdles despite Richard being very pessimistic about his chances each time. There's no doubt about Richard's talent as a trainer, but what had happened affected my confidence and we had a parting of the ways, although we remain on good terms. The Mr Lear story provides further confirmation, should any be required, that my horses are doing their best whether I've backed them or not.

Something that happened earlier, though, is still recollected with great amusement by my friends. Richard phoned me one day to say he'd received a letter addressed to me, care of the yard. It was a fan letter from a punter, who wrote that meeting me at Ascot a few years earlier had been the best day of his life. How nice of him to say so, I thought. In the next paragraph he went on to mention that his life had not been easy of late, as since our happy encounter at Ascot he had been sectioned! My friends have never let me forget that my only fan letter was sent by a madman.

CHAPTER 17

PICKING A
SUITABLE PILOT

THE vast majority of my punting takes place during the turf Flat season, but with the exception of my big Scoop6 win, the months straddling 2002-03 were by far my most profitable winter. Apart from Mr Pertemps, the other big contributor was The Baroness. Right from the start of her career, Stuart Williams warned me that she was fairly ordinary. However, The Baroness was genuine and we could hope to have a little touch somewhere down the line. She was green as a two-year-old and didn't achieve much in two starts over seven furlongs.

Stuart felt that she wasn't really thriving and said we should give her more time to mature. It was December before Stuart had her back in full training and by that point he was pretty sure she was a five-furlong horse. Her pedigree was a bit of a mixture, as her sire Blues Traveller was placed in the Derby yet she was a half-sister to Kathology, a decent sprinter. From her work at home it seemed that she would be following that side of the family. We took a crucial decision that would allow us to get outstanding value, and aimed for a little punt on her third run. It is a widely held opinion that many shrewd trainers campaign their horses with a view to winning once they have been allotted a handicap rating following the obligatory three runs. As a result, horses who have run twice for certain stables tend to be readily dismissed by those looking for a bet. In practice, the canniest trainers rely on knowing when a horse is coming into form rather than trying to formalise a plan too far in advance.

By dropping The Baroness down in distance for a Lingfield seller, we hoped that casual observers would assume we were interested in gaining a favourable mark for the future and search elsewhere for the winner. They would take one look at the trainer, compare the middle-distance sire with the five furlongs of the race, and dismiss us altogether. Often it's a case of outthinking the opponent. Sometimes it doesn't work, but on this occasion it was satisfying to see The Baroness among the longshots in a field of nine despite coming from a stable that was feared by the bookmakers.

I wasn't able to obtain a large bet in a selling race but, with an opening show of 50-1, it wasn't necessary. The Baroness touched 66-1 on-course, and was backed at all rates down to 12-1 before landing the punt by a length and three-quarters, resulting in a profit of £148,868 from a stake just short of £3,500 each-way.

That August, I nearly landed another big-priced touch at Chepstow with Disabuse. Having tried him at longer distances, Stuart thought he could pick up a little race back at seven furlongs, and confidence was quite high after some promising home gallops. Disabuse had been beaten a long way in his previous races and was completely unconsidered when the first show of 50-1 came through. We took all prices down to 20-1, resulting in an SP of 14-1, but second was the best he could manage. I ended up £27,373.75 in front thanks to the each-way money, but one place better would have produced a massive return.

One horse who only ever produced losses was Sleeping Elephant. The first bill was one of £44,000 for his purchase at the October yearling sales. I then sent the horse to William Haggas and waited until April before asking him about his ability. His reply stunned me. "I think he's Listed class at least," he said. I asked if this meant he was the best two-year-old in the yard, and William replied that he had one that was better called Dupont, who later won the German 2,000

Guineas and Italian equivalent. Sadly, Sleeping Elephant suffered a succession of injuries and despite the best efforts of first William and then Nigel Tinkler, he never saw a racecourse.

At the 2003 breeze-ups, I purchased a two-year-old by Miswaki for 30,000gns and sent him to Tim Easterby. More Sleepers, as we called him, was soon catching pigeons on the gallops and Tim was talking in terms that I had never heard him use before. Like most good trainers, he tends to be a pessimist and is never normally one to speak too confidently, but he was adamant that More Sleepers was better than anything in the stable. Word also reached me from elsewhere that the lads in the yard had been whispering about a US-bred machine of a two-year-old.

However, as in the case of Sleeping Elephant, injury struck just at the wrong time and More Sleepers was ruled out for the season after suffering a hairline fracture to his off-fore. There was always the doubt as to whether More Sleepers would be quite as good at three after his injury, but Tim reported that he was still working really well. In order to avoid reigniting memories of his scintillating work as a two-year-old and thus putting the kybosh on any sort of gamble, I renamed him Nistaki. To further draw a veil over the situation, we sent him to Vicky Haigh, a capable trainer with whom we could expect a big price in a maiden, as her profile was relatively low with the bookmakers.

Nistaki was all set for a seven-furlong contest at Folkestone in April. I'd seen his last piece of work before leaving Tim, when he'd smoothly taken care of Distant Times, a convincing winner at Warwick that month. The Folkestone race looked fairly moderate and I was keen to go for a big touch, especially at long odds. I spent some time lining up all the cannons for a punt on the opening show, as 25-1 hugely overestimated his chances. The bookmakers had been caught unawares and I stood to win close on £200,000, but in the event Nistaki ran well but could finish only fourth, so I got no return even on the each-way bets despite the horse being beaten less than two and a half lengths.

Sometimes I go to the sales convinced that I will buy a particular horse, only to come away empty-handed. Usually someone else just bids too much, but that was definitely not the case on one memorable occasion at Newmarket. At the October yearling sales in 2003, I very much liked the pedigree of a filly by the Derby winner Sinndar. Following the successes of Curfew, I had a big budget to buy a nice yearling to send to James Fanshawe, and was confident that a figure around the 100,000gns mark would capture her. I very rarely bid at the sales myself, as given that people know of my painstaking form study and relatively deep pockets, I see no need to advertise to them horses in whom I'm interested. I asked someone to bid for me, and when he nodded at my limit of 120,000gns, there was a long pause and it seemed that she was ours. I was very surprised when a further bid came in at 130,000gns, and stunned when I realised the winning bid had come from the vendor.

Over the next five minutes, the picture clarified. The vendor, Paul Arnold, heard that James Fanshawe was one of the underbidders. It can be embarrassing for a vendor when they bid higher than the anticipated sale price and buy the horse back, as it leads to suspicion that they are running-up the bidders. Paul rushed up to James, apologised for having bought-in the filly, and made it clear that he was open to agreeing a deal. He was at pains to stress that he had only placed the final bid because he had got wind that Patrick Veitch was buying the horse, and he didn't want her to go to a gambler.

In his upper-crust accent he used the word 'gambler' with a particular emphasis, clearly disapproving of the idea of anyone earning a living from backing horses. What Paul didn't realise, as he slated the idea of his filly being owned by the 'gambler' Patrick Veitch, was

Above: On the way to the races by helicopter.

Below: Collecting a trophy from Her Majesty The Queen (© Keith Robinson).

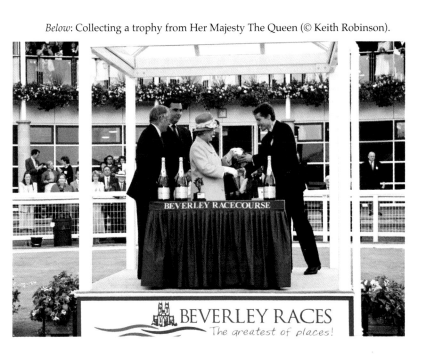

Above: Downland (red and light blue), backed from 66-1 to 40-1, lands the Tote Trifecta Handicap at Ascot in September 2001, having let us down badly three weeks earlier at Haydock when getting loose before the start (© racingfotos. com).

Below: Winning too far . . . Mr Lear about to face the handicapper's wrath having won a mile handicap at Southwell in February 2002 by sixteen lengths.

Unscrupulous gives me a first Royal Ascot winner in 2004. *Above*: jockey Oscar Urbina takes careful note of my instructions to spend as much of the race as possible on the favoured far rail (© Martin Lynch).

Below: Unscrupulous in the winner's enclosure (© Bernard Parkin).

The Exponential Coup, 100-1 to 8-1.
Above: The final furlong. The blinkers and eyeshield not only helped
Exponential (maroon) concentrate but convinced the betting market he was
one to avoid after he wore them on his racecourse debut six weeks earlier.

Below: On the way back in.

The gamble caused a media frenzy ranging from *The Sun* to *The Sunday Times,* including many full page articles away from the racing pages. Early suggestions within the betting world that there had been a sting were quickly squashed by the racing authorities who confirmed that everything was in order and that an 'old-fashioned gamble' had been landed.

Above: Sendintank, winner of ten handicaps the year before, wins again at the Doncaster St Leger meeting in 2005 (© Steve Parkin/PA).

Below: Zero Tolerance wins the first of two Listed races in 2006, holding Babodana by a head (© racingfotos.com).

Above: Pevensey (pink and yellow), backed from 16-1 to 8-1, gives me a second Royal Ascot winner in the 2007 Duke of Edinburgh Handicap.

Below: Enjoying a party.

Above: Silver Touch, the horse who took me over the £10 million profit mark when winning a Listed race at York in September 2006. This led to my decision to take time off in 2007-2008, giving me the opportunity to write this book.

Below: Agents normally report in by text message to reduce time spent on the phone.

that the person standing with James was none other than . . . Patrick Veitch. I made no comment whatsoever and allowed him to continue in full flow. James and I then wandered off to the cafeteria to laugh out loud at the episode. Over the next half-hour, word spread about the incident. Eventually, Paul came up to me to apologise profusely and say that he now wanted me to buy the horse after all. I didn't accept his offer, although we managed to put it behind us.

In racing, as in life, you need luck on your side. I've certainly had my share of good fortune but the dice haven't always rolled my way, and I still shudder at the story of the unluckiest loser I've ever had. I'm prepared to go even further by suggesting that the horse concerned could be the unluckiest loser anyone has ever had.

The horse concerned was Zero Tolerance, one of the best horses I've owned. He's won seven times, including two Listed races. On his only outing as a two-year-old he finished a promising sixth at Newcastle, so we then planned to take in a maiden on the all-weather in early 2003 before a campaign in some quality handicaps over the summer. Zero had been working brilliantly that first winter and David Barron told me that he was more than a match for any horse in the yard. A mile maiden at Southwell looked easy pickings, and a nice big field for a race in January ensured that we could expect a decent price. David had taken the precaution of giving Zero some invaluable practice on the course, so we knew there were no concerns about him handling the surface.

Keith Dalgliesh was engaged to ride. We were drawn towards the outside, 11 of 16 on the one-mile left-handed circuit at Southwell, which was good news. High numbers were favoured at this time as the inside of the track was riding slower. Of course, the lazier pundits would still assume that a wide draw was a disadvantage, on the assumption that the shortest way round a turning track was always the best way. The advantage of the draw also meant that instructions to the jockey could be very simple. All Keith had to do was ride to his stall position, stay reasonably handy and move into the lead up the straight. I did my bit by staking as much money as I could at all rates from 10-1 to 3-1.

What possessed Keith that day will remain a mystery for the rest of my time in racing. Right from the start, he appeared set on contravening his instructions. Step one in this horror story began when he chose to hold Zero up at the rear of the field, in direct contradiction to his orders. Zero is by Nashwan, he was going to stay the trip easily, so why on earth hang around at the back off an extremely slow pace?

Step two was just as bad. Keith failed to ride to his stall position. Instead, to my dismay, he attempted to manoeuvre towards the slower ground on the inside. No matter that he was riding for the man with by far the best record of any trainer at the track. Maybe someone had once told him that the inside route was the shortest route. Whatever the reason, clearly he felt that the top trainer at the course had it wrong.

Step three left me shaking my head in disbelief. Once he turned for home on Zero, Keith managed to stay in trouble towards the inside, which was still the slowest ground, for almost the whole length of the straight before frantically attempting to find a clear run. He finally extricated Zero Tolerance inside the final furlong. Pegasus would have struggled to make up the ground from such an unpromising position, but Zero was both willing and talented and his surging late charge took him to within a head of the winner, Saponi, at the line.

A truly dreadful ride had cost me close on £100,000 in winnings. Impartial observers would report that Zero Tolerance's ill-fortune in the straight made him look the unluckiest loser of the season. This was without even considering the massive damage that had been done in the first half-mile.

I've been driven to distraction by jockeys on a number of other occasions. A jockey should research the horse they are riding, the opposition, likely pace and draw, as well as which type of tactics have a recent record of success or failure on a particular course. In practice, this homework is all too often ignored as riders hurtle up and down motorways to fit in with their near-impossible schedules. I strongly believe that jockeys should be restricted to riding at one meeting a day. My reasoning for backing a horse is often greatly influenced by a nuance, or a key tactic, that I have spotted. If a jockey is not even aware of the basic evidence about the track that has been clear earlier in the afternoon, my bet may be scuppered before the stalls open.

Let's look at an extreme example of how detached from events jockeys can be in the hectic mid-summer. Take the Carlisle Bell meeting on June 28, 2006, the biggest day of the season at the track. This followed just nine days on from the previous fixture at Carlisle, when there had been a huge advantage in racing as wide as possible up the home straight. The track had not been watered, so without any doubt the assumption had to be that the stands' side would still be the place to be in the straight. In the first four races, how many jockeys headed for the stands' side? None.

Even after the first of two valuable handicaps had seen the widest-drawn horse win, not one jockey would recall the previous meeting and deduce that the stands' rail was the place to be in the second big race half an hour later. At what point did the penny drop? Not until the last race, when half the field came to the stands' side and slaughtered the far-side group, who were all beaten ten lengths or more in a seven-furlong race.

Who is the best jockey I've seen riding in Britain? Kieren Fallon. Would I ever use him? For my own reasons I'd prefer not to. Over recent years there has scarcely been an occasion on which I have used any of the jockeys who subsequently found themselves in hot water or were forced to serve lengthy suspensions. The only exception to this came when I allowed the trainer to use his stable jockey.

But if we ignore Fallon's conduct out of the saddle, why is he the most talented jockey? Crucially, he is supreme at judging pace and producing horses gradually to give them the best possible chance. He has the ability to take up exactly the right position in even the most high-profile races, when other top jockeys would settle for a happy medium. A fine example of this was his victory on Virginia Waters in the 2005 1,000 Guineas at Newmarket. The early pace was excessively strong. Aware that the leaders were going much too fast, Fallon sat way off the pace on Virginia Waters and was still last past halfway. When the others dropped away, having done too much too soon, he sauntered through and made his mount look a lot better than she actually was – she never won again – simply by judging the pace to perfection. In addition, Fallon's talent for winding horses up very gradually in their races is generally more effective than asking them for a sudden huge effort.

His other great skill is his ability to carry out difficult manoeuvres at any stage of a race. Take an example where it is important to move a horse on to a rail in order to race on the fastest ground. Most jockeys are able to attempt this manoeuvre for maybe a furlong, and then have to get on with riding a race. I have seen Fallon continue to try when it seemed impossible to do so and eventually work himself into the key position two or three furlongs later.

But, if it came to a choice, I'd overlook him and give narrow preference to Frankie Dettori over Jamie Spencer. Sadly, Frankie's availability is increasingly scarce these days as he rarely takes outside rides except at the major meetings. When available, though, he is supremely athletic in full flow on a racehorse, with great balance. He also has an excellent racing brain. Before a race, you can talk to him about, say, a technicality of the draw and he will understand completely and make intelligent comment. After the race his summaries are absolutely to the point. In the space of ten to 20 seconds he tells you everything you want to know.

I remember bumping into him on his way out of Nad Al Sheba racecourse at the end of Dubai World Cup night in 2003. He had won the big race by five lengths on Moon Ballad in such a style that many experts predicted that the horse would clean up around the world. I said: "Well done Frankie, that looked good." He replied: "Good horse *on this track*." His emphasis on the Nad Al Sheba track proved spot-on, as Moon Ballad failed to finish in the first four again before being retired.

On the same trip, I was having lunch outside one day, bumped into a few jockeys, including Frankie, and decided to share a table. As a heavy punter on the Flat, I think it is appropriate to limit my contact with Flat jockeys, but on holiday in the sun, while outside my working season, it wasn't a problem. I was soon being quizzed about my methods, the jockeys keen to hear about a different side to the sport. It was interesting that Frankie seemed most intrigued, taking it all in and asking perceptive questions, and he clearly remembered that conversation. Once or twice I've heard a shout of "Eh Pat, which side 'ere?" as Frankie prepared to walk out on to the course.

Spencer is outstanding at getting horses to relax and race efficiently, so that they expend the minimum amount of energy. Although he is known for holding horses up, he is very effective in front as well, as he has proved to great effect on Zero Tolerance. Some experts criticise him for holding up too many horses. In many cases they are just plain wrong, although there is perhaps the odd occasion where he could choose to change position earlier when the pace is not quite strong enough. If he embraces a little more flexibility then he has the potential to be the complete jockey. I could also nominate a couple of lesser-known jockeys, but I'm afraid that would make it a little too easy for the bookmakers to spot horses I owned when those riders were booked for stables associated with me.

Which jockeys would I not use? I shall exclude corruption issues, which have been well-documented elsewhere, as my input has to be limited without definitive proof. Of the higher-profile jockeys, I'd have to nominate Darryll Holland and Willie Supple. On those occasions where I have had personal experience, I have formed the impression that they had not taken on board some of the expertise that was available to them, which seemed to me to be unwise given their hectic schedules. One occasion that sticks in the mind was when Darryll rode a horse of mine called Uproar, trained by Ralph Beckett. Ralph and I were unimpressed with Darryll's effort and it would be the following year before his agent next rang Ralph for a ride, where-upon he got a considerable earbashing for his trouble.

Discretion is also a key factor in picking a suitable pilot. Jock-eys will often have knowledge based on home gallops, and it soon becomes clear if a certain pilot is talking out of turn. One rider in particular, who shall remain nameless, missed out on two Listed win-ners of mine after taking a less than diligent view on this subject. There tends not to be a second chance.

A horse of mine called Five Years On left myself and trainer William Haggas most unhappy after his third start at Southwell, for which he was odds-on favourite. After the race we were both most unhappy with the ride given by Carl Lowther. It is a fact that Lowther was dismissed from his job riding work for William following the incident.

Of course, comments from those who don't ride often attract strong criticism from those who do. Jockeys can and do get frustrated, but those who suggest that only those who have ridden are qualified to make expert comment are taking an absurd position. I recall watch-ing Tony McCoy firmly rejecting an opinion of Lydia Hislop quoted on Channel 4's The Morning Line by saying: "How many winners has she ridden?" I'm afraid that's not a very good criterion, Tony. You might be the best at riding horses, but I'm pretty sure the shrewdest judges of form in racing don't come from that group.

That's not to say that the media's viewpoint on jockeys is always a good one, and I'm afraid that many pundits view jockeys in simplistic terms. I'll provide the formula for a young jockey who wishes to attract prodigious praise from the media. First, wherever possible, take a position in about fourth place, towards the outside of the group. This should mean that you avoid trouble on the inside and also rarely get accused of misjudging the pace. Second, sit as still, and therefore 'cool', as possible until the two-furlong pole. Third, go for home and ride a polished finish.

Just to be clear, I am not saying that adopting these tactics is always a bad thing. The ability and willingness to sit still, for example, is a useful attribute, but the pundits are too easily impressed by jockeys who stick to this formula. Other equally important techniques tend to be overlooked. Issues that get far less attention include a) picking those races where the pace is too fast or slow and sitting about fourth is the wrong approach; b) developing the ability to safely make ground through a group of horses rather than needing to go the longer way round; c) appreciation of at least the basics of the draw; d) asking for an effort only gradually, allowing time for a horse to respond rather than changing straight from first gear into top. This last item is one of the most important, but is often still lacking in senior jockeys.

I'm sure many will disagree with parts of this chapter. Although I've had an awful lot of success betting on my opinions over the years, mine is only one view. Fortunately, I am a disciplined punter so I tend to get over disappointments quicker than most. One of my trainers a couple of years ago was furious with his jockey for ignoring instructions and instituting his own plan, despite having no prior knowledge of the horse. The trainer approached the stipendiary steward officiating that day and said: "If someone ever lets off a machine gun in the weighing room and takes them all out, don't bother to investigate it, just come and get me."

Okay, so that was something of an overreaction . . .

CHAPTER 18

"HERE . . . COMES . . . SEND . . . IN . . . TANK"

I LOST a far greater sum when Zero Tolerance ran at Royal Ascot in 2003. Having performed to a high level in steadily run races at a mile and a quarter, Zero seemed likely to improve significantly over a strongly run mile and a half. His half-brother High Pitched had won a Group 3 over a mile and five and Zero Tolerance was by a much stronger influence for stamina in Nashwan. He seemed sure to stay a mile and a half easily and it would be no surprise if he stayed much further than that. There you go – sometimes I get it completely wrong.

I plunged heavily on Zero in the King George V Handicap, staking a little over £50,000 at morning and afternoon odds. By the time I had finished I stood to win not far short of half a million pounds, but by the time he finished the race had been over for some time. He didn't come close to staying the trip and I had no-one to blame but myself.

Royal Ascot remained very much in my sights and Unscrupulous was my big chance in 2004. He was owned by Helena Springfield Ltd before I invested in him at the end of his four-year-old career. Although he was slow to progress in the spring, he had impressed when put into full work. He was still not fully wound up when appearing at Newmarket in late May under Frankie Dettori. Persuading Unscrupulous to relax in the early stages was the biggest problem by far and managing that in a seven-runner field with no early pace proved impossible, but he still ran well to finish third.

After that race Unscrupulous worked well, and James Fanshawe suspected that he was ahead of the handicapper. I felt that the recently introduced Buckingham Palace Handicap would suit him perfectly as a very strong pace was virtually guaranteed. However, a week before the meeting, James started to waver. He had warned me when I first came to the stable that he tended to get less confident as a race approached, and he was worried that our horse might need more experience, having only had seven races in his life. He suggested we might take in a small race first before going for bigger targets later in the season.

Entries for the Buckingham Palace closed Saturday lunchtime, so I sent James a detailed fax on the Friday evening, outlining why I felt we should go for a major handicap straight away. The fax did the trick and James was back on board with the Ascot plan. During the week, it was clear that a high draw was going to be important and I was delighted when we were drawn 23 of 30. On the day, the only issue for me was whether that stall would be high enough, as I knew that the quickest ground was close to the fair rail. I insisted that our jockey Oscar Urbina should switch behind the other runners to race tight against the far rail and stay there as long as he could. Oscar has had his critics, but he is very effective when riding a hold-up horse who needs to be settled and produced with a stealthy run late on.

I had taken the rare decision to add P Veitch to the partnership name. This was sure to attract plenty of attention on the day, but the odds would be out before then and, having dreamed of a Royal Ascot win for six years, I wanted to see my name in the racecard. My nightmare departure from Cambridge had happened only days after Royal Ascot in 1998, and I'd always thought a win at the meeting would be appropriate compensation.

I didn't have a huge bet, because James felt he was not value as one of the market leaders in a tough 30-runner handicap. Still, I knew we would be taking the best possible advantage of the draw and had a few thousand on at around 10-1. Having confirmed the instructions in the paddock, I had several minutes to kill before the race, so I phoned my parents and told them to turn the television on, as I might be having a winner at Royal Ascot. Oscar followed my instructions to the letter. After a furlong he was sat tight on the far rail, taking advantage of the quickest ground. The race was run at a strong gallop so his position in rear was no problem. He made steady progress through the middle section of the race and drew right away on Unscrupulous in the final furlong to win by five lengths. I'd achieved an objective set at my lowest point in 1998.

I made my way to the winner's enclosure and stood under the 'First' sign. I heard it said later that I was speechless at that point. That wasn't quite true. There was plenty I could have said, but I wasn't going to spoil the moment by babbling away with a few trite comments about how pleased I was. There would be plenty of time for celebrating later.

I was also pleased that the tactics we employed had contributed so much to the victory. That might sound ridiculous, as most racegoers seeing him win by five lengths would assume that he would have prevailed wherever he was drawn, but racing on that far-rail strip was worth more than five lengths. After Unscrupulous, who in effect raced from stall 30 of 30, the next five home from those racing on the far side were drawn 30, 29, 28, 26, 27. Their finishing positions were determined almost precisely by their stalls positions. Anyone still not convinced need only look at fifth-placed Peter Paul Rubens, drawn 20. Subsequent form proved that he was just as well handicapped as Unscrupulous that day, yet he was beaten eight lengths at Royal Ascot because he raced on slower ground. That's why I had £40,000 on him at Sandown next time out, winning £92,480.

Unscrupulous was plagued by injury after that and managed only one more run a year later, when he won at Newmarket. He was always a fragile horse and James did a marvellous job in coaxing him to that Royal Ascot win. That was his day.

The other ownership highlight of 2004 came from Sendintank, whose name was taken from an article in Private Eye some years earlier at a time when a new Chinese leader was due to be elected. The Chinese government is extremely enlightened on its policy of dealing with career criminals – they don't allow them at all. It is odd that most of their party are classed as moderates, despite an international reputation that is quite the opposite. The moderates are then divided into different factions, including the illogically named 'hardline moderates'. The Private Eye article parodied a whole range of candidates, from the 'moderate moderate' to the 'hardline no-nonsense whatsoever moderate' who was called Mr Sen Din Tank.

Sendintank was a good example of the patience I was prepared to employ before backing my judgement with hard cash. He was very immature at two, but Stuart Williams always felt he had a lot of potential, particularly when upped in trip. At three, he was never quite right, but that winter Stuart was far more impressed with The Tank. He was working like a decent horse and, with a rating of only 50, we felt a serious bet was warranted. The Tank returned to action at Wolverhampton less than two weeks into 2004. Ridden by Stuart's apprentice Brian Reilly and backed from 10-1 to 4-1, he sped home unchallenged, although the winning margin of 11 lengths left me flabbergasted at Reilly's tactics. He might just as well have sent a telegram to the handicapper telling him to pitchfork him up the ratings. Ian Mongan was crossed off my 'favoured jockeys' list in similar fashion, after Mr Lear landed a touch at Southwell. I am still amazed that Mongan managed to win by 16 lengths in a one-mile handicap despite being told to come late, in doing so incurring a major penalty from the handicapper.

Reilly was later involved in controversy in connection with a horse of mine called BA Clubman. He was only moderate but was making his debut in a shocking contest on the all-weather and was fancied to win. Stuart had taken the unusual step of trusting the jockey with the instructions in advance, but had told no-one else. It was a nasty shock, then, when one of my agents rang me and repeated the exact instructions that the jockey had been given, even down to the phrase 'don't win too far'. The fact that people in the betting industry had this news was hardly helpful, although BA Clubman was withdrawn before the race. Stuart and Reilly parted company soon afterwards with Reilly protesting his innocence, despite there being no other possible suspect. The fact that Reilly was later to have his licence suspended for passing information to a bookmaker, in races that took place less than 12 months later, rather put his denial into context. Maybe some of us were perhaps a little sharper than Reilly gave us credit for.

The Tank's victory was a few weeks before the BA Clubman incident, but it was an interesting warning sign that Reilly wanted to make extremely sure of victory. Perhaps coincidentally, when the betting shows had appeared, every move I made was a little too late. Maybe others were competing for my slice of the cake. My eventual winnings of £45,683 were much lower than I had been hoping for.

At that time it was still possible to win a succession of races within a period of up to 13 days, from Sunday to the following Friday, using the same handicap rating with only a single weight penalty of around 6lb for the first win. Sendintank won three times over the next 11 days, with each jockey under strict instructions to win cheekily and all three managing to win by less than two lengths, thus keeping the handicapper's wrath within reasonable bounds. The Tank was then given a break. We were keen to make the best possible use of his handicap rating and he was now rated lower on turf than on the all-weather. He would be able to race off a rating of 60 in a turf race, only 10lb higher than the rating on which he had started the year.

The Tank reappeared in April. Stuart's horses endured a miserable time in the first half of that turf season, so we picked the most competitive race we could find for Sendintank and just sent him out to do his best. We were delighted when he finished third at Pontefract, as Stuart felt he could improve radically once his horses came back to form. Again, I would point out that by clearly making a positive effort, we ensured that there wasn't a whole string of pundits forecasting big things for him on turf.

Once Stuart's horses found their sparkle on the racecourse, it was time to wheel The Tank back into battle. We chose a handicap at Yarmouth in late August, and it turned into one of those heady days when I just wanted to get on as much money as possible. This was going to be far from easy, as the bookmakers had taken a tremendous kicking from a whole array of other touches in the previous weeks. They were stampeding for cover at the first sign of Veitch activity – there go the wildebeest – but as long as they didn't know which horse I was going to back, there were still some moves I could make.

Staying one step ahead of the bookmakers has often included the use of what I call 'guile' accounts. The firms like to place a 'mark' against successful accounts. They use the clues obtained from marked accounts to make rapid adjustments to their prices. However, making dramatic reactions to small bets comes with risks attached. I have long been in the habit of converting a series of marked accounts, giving them 'guile' status.

These accounts are then used purely to create a false trail, causing a market move for a horse I don't fancy, while making it easier to place larger bets on the horse I actually want to back. The method is particularly effective with those bookmakers who seem keen to place large bets themselves when they believe that a horse is hot. Betting activity on a selection of guile accounts then leads to thousands of pounds changing hands as the greedy bookmakers in question try to place much larger bets than they have been willing to lay to their clients. Such horses frequently collapse in the betting, causing more interesting runners to drift out to very attractive prices. In recent years, one very well-known offshore firm have been particularly guilty of operating a 'lay small, bet large' policy, and have been regular recipients of guile business. As I write, their activities continue, and they can expect increasingly regular use of this method in the future.

It isn't always necessary to actually place bets on a guile account. Back in the early days, I was all set for a huge bet at Kempton on Art Of War in the Listed Sirenia Stakes, as I was convinced he would easily take care of his chief market rival Princely Heir. I knew that plenty of others would be keen to back Art Of War, but felt there would be strength in the early-price market. Prices were not due out until 10.15, so right at the beginning of the trading day I arranged for all manner of guile-account-holders to request an ante-post price about Princely Heir for the following year's 2,000 Guineas. It didn't matter that most of the clients didn't take the price they were offered. The mere fact that there was a flood of phone calls interested in Princely Heir's chance of winning a race in the very top division was enough to ensure he was priced up very defensively.

Sure enough, when the betting came out, Princely Heir opened up too short in the betting with Art Of War, who should have been red-hot favourite, a similar price. Art Of War was the subject of huge support all day and eventually started even-money favourite. The support was justified as he won comfortably. I heard one report of a bookmaker cursing the clowns who had enquired about the Guineas price on Princely Heir. The willingness of bookmakers to get carried away with only the tiniest amount of business never fails to charm me, and by keeping note of those accounts that cause the greatest over-reaction it is often easy to start the ball rolling in the wrong direction.

Back to Sendintank. At Yarmouth, our supposed danger was the Sir Mark Prescott contender Lawrence Of Arabia. Sir Mark is a master trainer, but as his horse had been an unplaced favourite twice in the last month, I was confident he would discover that tanks operate very effectively in the desert. Nonetheless, a few carefully placed investments by the troops on Lawrence Of Arabia in the morning caused some sharp operators to wrongly believe that they knew which of the pair was fancied. The opening show of 2-1 Lawrence Of Arabia, 4-1 Sendintank was something to behold.

The SP of 2-1 Sendintank, 9-4 Lawrence Of Arabia perhaps offered some clues about the dangers of bookmakers over-reacting to small amounts of early money. Lawrence Of Arabia was never sighted as Sendintank stormed home by five lengths, with Neil Callan trying hard to prevent him from winning by any further. A profit of £63,604.18 was very satisfactory considering the run I'd been having, and the fact that the horse was viewed with caution by the industry after landing that earlier gamble.

We had remembered to start The Tank off at the beginning of a week, so he was able to run up three more wins over the next ten days at Newmarket, Newcastle and Haydock. The odds were inevitably much shorter by now, but in my view he was still a little overpriced each time and I collected small winnings totalling £38,824.58 over the three races. He was also becoming a really popular horse with punters as he had won eight out of nine for the year, seven of them as favourite, each time coming from off the pace.

Sendintank recorded his eighth win at Haydock on the Friday. He stayed overnight at the track and the next afternoon had the task of running in a much tougher race – the £50,000 Old Borough Cup – off a new rating of 82, a stone higher than before. We were hopeful rather than confident, yet he would have made it but for meeting with bad luck in the straight before failing by a length to catch the winner. It was a gritty display that showed he hadn't finished winning for the season. Stuart had once again proved his skill as a trainer in having Sendintank in such terrific condition that he could race at his peak five times in 12 days. Now the horse needed another break before coming back for one further burst before the end of the Flat season. We wanted to make an assault on the record for the number of handicap wins in a season, which stood at 11. Sendintank could equal that record if he managed three more victories, so we mapped out a trio of targets over five days early in November.

The Tank duly won at Musselburgh on November 3 before heading to Doncaster on the final day of the turf season to attempt win number ten. Under a further penalty for Musselburgh he now had a rating of 91 to contend with, but proved equal to the task as he prevailed by half a length. To put together ten successes in a season, all in handicaps, you need a sound and resolute horse, a degree of good fortune, and jockeys who understand the necessity of winning their races by narrow margins. We had managed this apart from Reilly's lapse at Wolverhampton at the start of the year.

One of the best parts of the day at Doncaster was watching Sendintank's lad cheer him on in the closing stages. Tak was over from Japan for a year and spoke very little English, but he roared him home all the way up the straight with repeated cries of "KO-ON-TANK". Commentator Mark Johnson was in raptures as he called the final furlong, the words "HERE . . . COMES . . . SEND . . . IN . . .TANK" shouted at maximum volume with pauses between each word. The punters' favourite had won again and was now nine from nine when heading the betting.

After triumph, disaster. Sendintank was due to go for the record on the Monday, two days after Doncaster, and would have been able to race off the same rating as on the Saturday but in a slightly lower grade on the first day of the all-weather season. However, the authorities had chosen to change the declaration time to 48 hours instead of 24 from that very day, so we needed to declare on the Saturday instead of Sunday. Unfortunately, Stuart was away and a mistake was made, with the depressing result that The Tank was not declared for Monday. He would surely have started odds-on to win his 11th race of the season.

The record attempt was still on, but the two races that remained open to us allowed time for the handicapper to react to his latest successes, and Sendintank was raised a further 5lb to a mark of 96. Both races were over a mile and a half, sharper than ideal for him on the tight all-weather tracks, and Sendintank would run bravely to finish a close third – to the same horse, Hello It's Me – each time. He had enjoyed a marvellous and profitable campaign but fate had conspired against him just as the record was within his grasp.

The following season, The Tank put up some fine efforts in higher grades, finishing third in a Listed handicap at York before returning to the Knavesmire for the Ebor. Martin Dwyer, who had won three times on The Tank, was back on board but I felt he rather overdid the waiting tactics that day and, after meeting trouble up the straight, looked unlucky not to go close, finishing seventh behind Sergeant Cecil, who was having his own annus mirabilis that season. Next time out, in a handicap at the St Leger meeting at Doncaster, Jamie Spencer got him home by three-quarters of a length from Cristoforo, trained by Barney Curley.

So to Newmarket two weeks later for a Listed race, the first non-handicap The Tank had run in since he was a two-year-old, and we felt he was a contender without being confident. He ran very creditably in third, but it proved to be the saddest of days as he never made it back to the unsaddling enclosure. Sendintank had broken down badly and stayed out on the racecourse, where he received attention from the racecourse vets. There was some doubt initially as to whether he would survive the next 24 hours, so it was a huge relief when he made it back home safely. The injury was too severe to keep him in training and soon it was time to find him a new home. He is now enjoying a happy retirement at my friend Lucy Watson's family farm in Yorkshire, where he is very well cared for.

I can't talk about most of my horses from very recent times as the bookmakers would no doubt be interested in up-to-date information of my activities. A second win at Royal Ascot, however, is enough for me to break cover given the special significance I'd attached to winning there. Pevensey, in 2007, was the horse to do it.

As mentioned earlier, I'd bought him the previous October, having been asked by Martin Green and a group of his golfing friends to include them in a syndicate to buy a dual-purpose horse. The Horses in Training Sale at Newmarket was clearly the place to look and I had studied the catalogue hard. Pevensey stood out, as he was very well treated on his win at Ascot a few weeks earlier. That had been one of the strongest handicaps of the season and the form certainly indicated that Pevensey's rating of 90 was on the lenient side. Two subsequent defeats were easily explained, as he had not appreciated a very slow pace at Ascot on the first occasion and didn't appear to relish the all-weather surface at Lingfield next time.

Those two efforts had taken the sting out of his value, but a few days before the sale I heard the disappointing news that he'd been withdrawn. However, I was so keen on the horse by this stage that I wasn't prepared to give up the chase. One door had closed so I chose another route, putting Geoffrey Pooley on the case to make a private offer. His first bid of £70,000 was rejected by the Buckley family, who owned and trained him. When we upped the offer to £80,000, we had a deal. Pevensey won twice for us over hurdles during the winter, but I was already looking ahead with keen anticipation to the summer, aware that his very best form was at Ascot and that the Duke of

Edinburgh Handicap at Royal Ascot was over his perfect distance of a mile and a half.

John Quinn has been a top trainer under both codes in recent years and had the job of getting Pevensey spot-on for Royal Ascot. The horse was not an exuberant worker at home, so John had to rely on his instinct rather than concrete gallop calculations to gauge his progress. By early June, he was reporting that the signs were positive. On the day, the bookmakers focused too closely on Pevensey's finishing position at York on his reappearance the previous month rather than on his outstanding course form. At York, he'd made a poor start, an annoying habit that has spoiled his chance on a number of occasions. He'd also found the distance too short that day. To my surprise and delight (and eventual financial reward) he was 16-1 with most firms in the morning. It quickly became clear that many others fancied his chances, and we had to move swiftly to secure the best odds as the price tumbled to his eventual SP of 8-1.

Pevensey was drawn on the wide outside in stall two, a bad draw in the public's eyes, but I knew it would not be a problem for him on slow ground at Ascot. If anything, it was an advantage. The only difficulty was having enough time to pass on my instructions to Graham Gibbons, as my co-owners were rather more concerned with taking photos in the paddock than allowing me to talk tactics with our jockey.

Pevensey was held up as usual in the early stages and stayed wide as planned. From there, Graham made stealthy progress mid-race before leading in the straight and just holding on in a desperate finish by a head and a short head from Solent and Hitchcock. A second Royal Ascot win was in the bag. The post-race celebrations lasted for many hours and we were among the last to leave the track. Sadly, two members of the syndicate, Martin and Doug, were unable to make it, as a potential winner at Royal Ascot was not deemed a sufficiently pressing engagement to allow a release from family commitments. At a subsequent celebration dinner, I made the light-hearted suggestion that the two might be slightly henpecked. My accusations were refuted at the next social gathering, with both parties reporting that they were to deny any such suggestions following strict instructions from their bosses back home.

Owning horses has provided me with the twin benefits of enormous entertainment and plenty of profit. I might not make money quite as quickly as when just studying the form, but it certainly adds much variety and spice to my daily jousts with the bookmakers. Finally, I've been asked whether I was anything to do with the gamble on Big Secret, who was backed from 33-1 to 7-1 when winning a bumper at Exeter in October 2006? I'm afraid that has to stay a big secret!

CHAPTER 19

PREPARATION

I'VE KEPT one ownership story back until the very end of this section. Of all the coups I've landed, the punt on Exponential on August 16, 2004 at Nottingham was the most dramatic and certainly attracted the most publicity. The gamble from 100-1 to 8-1 is, as far as I'm aware, the largest tumble in odds, during the pre-race shows, about a winner in the UK. The betting shows in the final ten minutes before a race are the most important by far. Before that, bookmakers put up a variety of flaky odds that can disappear in seconds, but once the show appears, the same price is available everywhere. Experience has taught them that they can lay these odds with more confidence, as there has been plenty of time to adjust for moves in the market.

Exponential was bought at the Doncaster two-year-old breeze-up sale in the spring of 2004. Breeze-up auctions are different from other sales in the UK, as the horses, who are all unraced, gallop in public before the sale. Over the previous few seasons, I had used a method that allowed me a tremendous edge at these sales. Most buyers would use their eyes to see which horses were impressive, although at the Newmarket breeze-up stopwatches were available, allowing timing between the furlong markers. However, taking furlong-marker timings is far from easy to do accurately from a distance, or even from the TV pictures. It was clear that very few buyers had access to accurate timings. This contrasted with American breeze-ups, where exact sectional times were published.

It was obvious that having precise times would be a considerable advantage, so from 2000 onwards, I took a team of my agents and placed them at five positions along the track. By co-ordinating stopwatches to start at exactly the same time, and recording the split time as a horse went past them, it was possible to produce extremely accurate sectional times. Nothing was left to chance; each agent was even given a spare stopwatch. The strategy paid rich dividends and I bought a steady stream of winners for knockdown prices. By far the most remarkable was the purchase of Curfew at Newmarket in 2001. She ran six lengths quicker over two furlongs than any other horse that day, yet I managed to buy her for only £21,000.

The downside was that our activities attracted considerable attention. The timers had a visible presence and the need to watch videos of the breezes while processing figures on a laptop attracted further scrutiny. In 2001, we walked away with two serious horses, bought for much less than other lots were making. Our status as pioneers couldn't last, and a legion of timers appeared in subsequent years. In 2005, representatives of Sheikh Mohammed's son Rashid bought heavily at the sales using a timing-based strategy. Suddenly, horses I had been buying for £20-30,000 were being bought less selectively, yet making £100,000+. As a result, the value of the timings has been eroded, and I have to be far more selective at these sales now, relying on my skills as a racereader.

There were still a few pickings left in April 2004 at Doncaster, where I bought a dark bay colt by Prix de l'Abbaye winner Namid for £27,000. I sent him to be trained by Stuart Williams, who had helped in the selection process. As with nearly all my horses, a partnership was registered, including Geoffrey Pooley and a few others.

At the sale, there had been quite a lot of banter among friends and trainer Ralph Beckett had been coming in for some stick. Geoffrey had known him since school and had been best man at his wedding. Stuart and I had long contended that the word Ralph was correctly pronounced with a short 'a' as in, say, Ralph Lauren, whereas those from the top public schools favoured the rather stranger version, as in Ralph Fiennes. Anyway, by the end of a lively session in a Doncaster curry house, things had degenerated to the point where Ralph had been renamed Rolph Bucket. On the way back to London, we decided to name the horse 'Rolph' under the partnership of 'The Bucketeers' with, of course, his namesake to be left unawares until the horse made its debut.

A few weeks later, Stuart told me that the colt was promising and that there was a chance we would land a touch if we allowed him time to mature. This caused a rethink on the naming situation. Rolph had seemed a good idea after the fun of the sales, but now that we might have business to do there was no value in alerting too many people to the horse. If even a few 'faces' in the betting industry deduce a horse is mine, the odds are dramatically affected. Rolph became Exponential, named after a trading term I used.

As I mentioned in the Sendintank story, Stuart's horses made a very quiet start to the 2004 turf season. Dealing with a period like this is made much easier for his clients by his complete frankness. Owners tend to remain with the stable for many years because they know Stuart does not wear rose-tinted glasses when assessing or describing his horses, reporting any concerns as soon as they arise. Those who like a bet also appreciate that Stuart is insistent that the owner of the horse is the priority and should not have to compete with others in securing his price. The only difficulty as an owner is that the trainer is so open about his concerns that in a particularly frustrating period he can seem to be excessively pessimistic. His Newmarket neighbour William Haggas often gives him a ribbing about this and has nicknamed him 'Grumble'.

Stuart felt Exponential was ready for his first outing in high summer, although at the time his horses were woefully out of form. It was assumed that there was some sort of virus affecting them, but it is often hard to nail down an exact cause. Stuart was adamant that

Exponential was not unwell, however, and would need a run to get the hang of things. Some horses learn about racing naturally, whereas many need experience before they know their job, so Exponential headed to Beverley for his first outing in July, a five-furlong two-year-old maiden.

Stuart felt that as the horse was a quirky character he was likely to need some sort of headgear to make him concentrate enough to fulfil his potential. Blinkers may stop an erratic horse being distracted, but bookmakers are well aware of the merits of this tactic so they tend to be more cautious about horses wearing such headgear for the first time. It is normal to give a horse the benefit of the doubt at the very beginning of a career, then add headgear if he subsequently proves difficult. Using headgear on a horse's debut is an extreme tactic and is likely to affect any resale value, as it creates the image of a way-ward type. Nevertheless, I was happy to fit headgear straight away. Although we were losing the chance to produce extra improvement at a later date, we would avoid giving the clue of 'first-time blinkers' on such an occasion. Stuart also felt that an eyeshield wouldn't go amiss, so we added that for good measure, arguably raising further questions about the horse's attitude.

With his yard in the middle of a barren spell and equipped with both blinkers and an eyeshield, Exponential was completely unfan-cied both by the stable and the racing public, and started at 25-1 at Beverley. He showed some early speed but, despite being given every chance by jockey Vince Halliday, fell away tamely in the latter stages of the race and came in last of the 13 runners.

At this stage, it is important to point out that our jockey gave him positive encouragement to get involved in the race. It may be perceived that someone with betting in mind might want their horse held up at the back of the field and given little encouragement. As I've said before and will say again, this is not something I believe in.

The fact that Vince very clearly asked Exponential to be competitive before the horse dropped away would avoid press write-ups about a 'promising' first run. As has often been the case, by following the rules I would end up with a bigger price. When racereaders' reports were published, the bait about the blinkers had been taken. Timeform commented that he was 'disconcertingly fitted with headgear on his debut'. As he had finished last, punters were going to be itching to oppose him next time.

Over the next few weeks, Stuart's stable began to return to form. Viral problems often seem to go as quickly as they appear. After the first winner on July 15 ended a drought stretching back to early May, there were another five winners by the end of the month. In Newmarket, Exponential was making terrific strides in his work. Stuart felt he was ready for another run at the end of the month and hinted that we had chances of winning at long odds. His horses tend to improve gradually with racing, with the result that many of them need a few runs before they manage to win. Stuart felt he had found a very fast learner who might defy normal expectations.

At this point, I took the crucial decision to delay Exponential's second run for a week or two. I wanted to be sure. We already knew enough to have a bet at long odds and often it is wise to strike when a horse seems right, but I sensed that Stuart was warming to the horse by the day and if we waited a little longer we might really have something to go to war with. I suggested another couple of tests at home before a race in mid-August.

The plan paid off. Stuart called a week later to say that he now thought Exponential could make up into the best horse I'd owned. His work had been outstanding and Stuart felt he could win a maiden without difficulty. We decided on a five-furlong contest at Nottingham on Monday, August 16. The Ebor meeting at York, the feature event of the month, started the following day. Punters and bookmakers would be far more interested in looking ahead to York than sniffing around for information in little races at Nottingham, trying to find out what I didn't want them to know. Although I tend to have my horses in stables that are fairly secure, there are always risks that information will leak out.

On the preceding Saturday, I carefully looked through the likely runners. There were plenty of horses with decent form, but on closer inspection none of them looked seriously promising. This was perfect, as Stuart only felt that we needed to avoid a really strong contender, and the fact that several had proper form would make it easy to rule out our horse. On this occasion, Stuart's reputation as a shrewd operator would count in our favour, as he was rightly respected as a trainer who did well in handicaps. Knowing that he didn't win many maiden races, tipsters and form students would be swift to write off Exponential's chance of success. Similar thinking had led them astray when The Baroness landed her punt a year earlier.

Stuart didn't have a stable jockey at the time and we needed a capable rider who would not attract a lot of attention. David Allan was attached to Tim Easterby's yard and had been riding well without being noted as fashionable. He looked an ideal choice. I called Stuart on the Sunday evening. He wasn't pessimistic this time. He believed we had a horse who might progress to Listed company the following season, and suggested that my betting strategy should be a simple one. I should get as much money on as I could manage at whatever price was available, with no lower limit. Given that early forecasts were around 50-1 there seemed no danger of the price going too low, but I confirmed exactly what he meant by asking: "So even if the price is cut to something ridiculous like 5-2, will I continue to smash away?" "Yes," he replied. An interesting day lay ahead.

CHAPTER 20

THE COUP

S TUART had given his bet to me and I would handle bets for other members of the partnership. I have always made a point of trying to group all the business together. I have witnessed some fumbling efforts by others to land a coup, and it is remarkable that so many attempts are ruined by those involved acting in an uncoordinated manner.

There was no danger of my making the trip to Nottingham. The off-course betting market was much larger and course bookmakers love to attach importance to who they see at the races. I learned that early on and have never been one for being seen on a day when a carefully laid plan was unfolding. On one occasion, a social visit to Ripon had sparked a huge punt on an unfancied runner from a stable with which I was associated. A domino effect had occurred as 'informed' sources scrambled to capitalise on the so-called news that I had been seen at the races. Instead, I planned everything from the office. When people quiz me about my betting, they often ask where my agents go to put the bets on, whether they use telephone, internet, betting shops etc. The answer is that I will aim to hit the bookmakers everywhere during a large bet, rather than focusing on one outlet.

The prime threat to a gamble inevitably comes from trusting others. In an ideal world, I would spend the hours leading up to a race preparing all manner of people for the business ahead. In practice, it only needs one agent to place too much trust in someone close to them and everything can be ruined. It is no solution to withhold the name of the horse or the race time. The mere whisper that 'something is on today' can go round the betting world in minutes and leave dozens of people in the industry waiting by the phones, ready to jump straight in and take their share of the action. So I couldn't forewarn my agents that business was pending. It would just seem like any other day to anyone calling my office.

Geoffrey Pooley and The Robot had a higher security rating, so would be given a few hours' notice to get ready and a rough idea of the type of business we would be doing, although not the name of the horse. They were the two agents who had the best record on security matters. The race was at 2.45pm. At a small meeting on a Monday, betting shows normally appear no more than eight to ten minutes before the off. From 1.30pm onwards I laid out my desk for the operation.

First, I prepared the phones. I had a dedicated mobile number allowing incoming calls for each of the agents. When the time came, I could then send a group text message, advising them all to call me at the same time. There were also spare phones for one-off use by occasional agents who would be assigned a number on the day. In all, there were 14 mobiles on my desk plus six landlines on a digital switchboard. I then created my checklist, underlining each item that would need my attention and the specific time that I would deal with it. These would be written in note form to save time.

1.55pm Bet check. A full rundown of internet sites to keep an eye on betting activity. All the signs indicated that there was no interest in Exponential, but it was vital to keep checking. If he suddenly attracted attention it would cause me to act differently. If a horse starts to look hot in the betting, there's a far greater risk of a price collapse, and it would be worth taking the chance of giving everyone more warning to make sure they could all pounce the moment the 'show' came through. If everything stayed quiet, I could give very little warning, to minimise the chance of a leak.

2.00pm GP. Check in with Geoffrey, to ensure his accounts were ready.

2.05pm CR. The same check with The Robot.

2.10pm Bet check. Go through the checklist again on the basis that time spent on reconnaissance is never wasted. Some might find my attention to detail obsessive, but with a coup like this you can never be too careful. I would be checking the betting more frequently than 15-minute intervals, but the 15-minute point was the time for a full review of all relevant sites.

2.14pm Nott. I had to watch the first race at Nottingham, which was run over the same course and distance, to check for any surprises from the draw.

2.18pm. Trainer. Last call to finalise David Allan's instructions after seeing the first race. It had passed without incident, while confirming our view that our middle to high draw offered a slight advantage. Tactics were fairly simple. Stuart felt that trying to hold Exponential up would not be successful as he was quite headstrong, so the plan was to allow him to race handily. David could then pick his own point to strike for home.

I wrote 'trainer' rather than Stuart's name. If I was planning a bet I'd often have to organise important decisions from more public places, maybe a table in the restaurant at a major meeting. With that in mind, out of habit, I'd never write things down that would give too much away to prying eyes.

2.20 to 2.33pm. Individual time slots to contact all the agents involved. The group text for main agents was sent at 2.30pm, but there would be additional calls to prepare other agents that I used more occasionally. I wouldn't get hold of everyone I tried, but there was a large enough pool of people to call on. It is possible to flood the market with too many bets, so I didn't need to reach everybody. For a smaller bet, the whole process of communicating with agents would be handled by Geoffrey, but I supervised the largest bets myself.

Each agent would be given a separate timeslot. Those not part of the group text message would start off with a timeslot marked 'R', meaning a call at that time to 'ready' them that business is pending. Once readied, agents would then be assigned a new time, with an 'O' indicating that this is the time to get them 'on the line' by telephone. Many agents would have their own sub-agents so would need slightly longer between their 'R' and 'O' times.

How were things shaping up in the market? From a betting point of view, Exponential was in a coma. On Betfair, he was out to 179-1, and the first show from the course came in at 100-1. Subsequent press enquiries discovered that on-course he was priced at 100-1 on most boards, with a couple at 125-1.

The press thereby dispelled the first myth that went around in the days after the race, that 100-1 was not the true price from the course. Betting is a business that seems to have a huge share of the world's green-eyed monsters. There is a second myth that has grown with the passing of time. It was decided in certain quarters that the opening show was in some way affected by fake movements on the internet, that the 179-1 wasn't a real price. Hundreds of thousands of pounds, sometimes millions, are traded on every race, every day on Betfair. I had a look at the amount traded on Exponential just before the first show. From memory, the figure was £8.

This was an incredibly small total to be bet on a horse in around 18 hours of trading. Such a horse was guaranteed to reach a massive price, as those traders who tried to lay small bets on perceived no-hopers battled with automatic betting machines – 'bots' – to offer a steadily bigger price. So the actual cause of the 100-1 first show was the unique combination of circumstances that caused no-one to bet on Exponential, even at huge odds, except for the £8. We had a horse who was written off on form, on his premature headgear and the trainer's past record. A watertight stable and owner ensured that no-one had sprung the trap early.

At around 2.35pm, it was time to go to work. In the preceding minutes, I had succeeded in contacting the required number of agents and they were now all on the line. I shouted out a bet of '£80 each-way times your multiplier' with a minimum price of 16-1, which would allow plenty of scope for bets after the price started to fall. Each agent had a 'multiplier' that would be changed only rarely during the season, reflecting their different strengths. A small agent might have a multiplier of 3 and be seeking a bet of £240 each-way, whereas the largest agent had a multiplier of 30 and was seeking £2,400 each-way. After everyone had rung off to get started, it was time for three final calls to riskier agents who I preferred not to forewarn at all. A massive gamble was now underway.

With about eight minutes to go, what action do I take at this point of a major bet? In fact, I often have nothing to do, because the time needs to be spare in case of communication problems. Everything had gone smoothly, so I had nothing to occupy me for two or three minutes. A peculiar sense of calm hit me. Perhaps the best analogy is that of a submarine commander after he has launched a torpedo. They can take many minutes to reach their target, and after the launch there's not much to do except wait. I knew that the betting industry would be on fire within two minutes, as bookmakers became aware of the gamble and frantically tried to take cover. There would also be the sheep of the betting world who would realise that something was happening and attempt to join in.

It was vital that the price of 100-1 lasted a few minutes but not too long. With the liabilities involved, the betting on Exponential would very quickly have reached a point where nearly every bookmaker in the land would turn away further bets at 100-1. Having obtained plenty of 100-1, we needed the odds to get down to a less alarming level so that the second wave of business could commence. Once the price had fallen heavily there were bookmakers willing to take further bets, thinking that the 'value' had now gone. A second wave of bets was now placed by my agents at 33-1, 20-1 and 16-1.

In the final minutes, it was time for the third wave. After the price had fallen below the agents' minimum of 16-1, it was time to move in on the internet. With the advent of betting exchanges, the business is full of punters looking to trade by laying a horse at shorter odds than the price they had already taken. Now it was time to turn the work of all the followers to my advantage.

A follower, maybe a bookmaker's employee who has phoned another bookmaker and 'nicked' £100 at 33-1, might now choose to lay £300 at 10-1 on the internet, so that he stands to make a £200 profit if the bet loses and £300 if it wins. Helpful to the end, I was there to accommodate them, knowing that at 10-1 I was still getting an absolute steal. It was during this third wave that the phone calls and texts came back from agents. I scribbled their reports down and could tell that business had gone well.

At Nottingham, Stuart had saddled Exponential and now waited in the racecourse Tote shop for the action to start. He was delighted that a horse carrying so much confidence not only opened at 100-1, but was still that price when the runners reached the start. Security had been perfect. He even panicked for a moment, wondering whether I had been distracted in the final few minutes and failed to place the bets. As the odds finally began to tumble, William Haggas, standing nearby, asked him: "What's all this about?" Stuart gave nothing away, shrugging his shoulders and replying: "No idea."

And, after all the planning and preparation, the months leading up to the day and the hectic machinations on the day itself, the race. It was over in 61.72 seconds. Exponential was soon close to the leaders and looked to be travelling well, with David sitting quietly. As the runners passed halfway, quite a few of the jockeys behind were hard at work, but David and Exponential were still travelling smoothly.

David eased Exponential into the lead just after the two-furlong marker and from that point on never really looked like being headed, although the last furlong seemed to last longer than normal. By 2004, I had honed to the limit my skills of staying calm, but I'll admit my heart may have been beating just a little faster for this final 12 seconds. Exponential had done it. We had done it. He held on by a length and all the planning had been worthwhile.

I started totting up the numbers immediately. First, I had to confirm a few figures with Geoffrey. All the bets had been returned to me and he had a share of my bets. The phase three exchange betting is not normally part of such a bet, as it was rare that we wanted to press on after a price had been savaged, so it was greatly amusing when he replied "HOW much?" when I called over just how much we'd won from phase three. When all the calculations had been completed, the winnings on my sheet came to £327,929.03, which included the stable business and that of my trading manager. My share came to £235,133.71.

What was the total sum won? Well, having spoken to most of the agents involved, I can confidently state that our total was very close to £500,000. If including the bets of those who followed in on the gamble, I would guess that the total won on Exponential was somewhere north of £1 million. I don't think that being a follower is a good policy in general, as these days the markets move in all sorts of strange ways and just following the ones that shorten is very dangerous, but on this occasion anyone that did take the hint was certainly happy.

It was not a bad day's work for me, and I write that prime piece of understatement with a grin on my face. I'm sure there have been people who have won a lot more on a race, perhaps even on a quiet Monday, but not with the track record that I had on that day. At the time, I was in the middle of a thunderstorm. In the previous three weeks alone (July 26-August 15) I had made more than £800,000, thanks to an incredible week at Glorious Goodwood that had netted me more than £400,000. What's more, over the previous 18 months, my winnings were getting on for £4 million. This made me about as much of a marked man as it was possible to be, and made the job of getting my bets on very much harder.

The media pounced on the gamble within minutes of the horse crossing the line. Racing UK were covering the meeting and immediately set to work reviewing the situation. Sure enough, they swiftly dug out the video of his previous race at Beverley and reviewed it for clues to the gamble. This suited me fine, as it was plain to see that Vince Halliday had not put a foot wrong at Beverley. That killed off any suggestion that we had broken the rules in setting up the sting.

At York's Ebor meeting over the next three days, the gamble was a constant source of interest, and David Nicholls was one of the first to offer his congratulations. Talking to him allows a 5' 10" person to get an insight into what life would be like as a 7ft basketball player, as I'm sure David won't mind me saying that he's about as tall as the average bar stool and that you have to tilt your head right forward to look him in the eye! Although the rumour mill suggested I was behind the gamble, I wasn't planning to give anything away to him or anyone else, so feigned surprise when David brought up the subject. David is no fool, though, and carried on regardless with his congratulations.

It was a hectic week in terms of press attention. In addition to mass coverage in the *Racing Post*, there were full-page articles in the *Daily Mail*, *Daily Express* and *The Sun*, and stories in many other papers. By the Thursday, I assumed that things had quietened down, but I received a call from a contact in the betting industry warning that he had heard that *The Sun* were planning a second big article on the gamble, this time naming me as the mastermind behind it. The call put me on red alert, so when a news agency called me half an hour later I was even more guarded than usual.

Another full-page article appeared in *The Sun* the next day but without mention of my name, although I was named in the Post, who quoted my stonewall defence in which I refused to confirm or deny my involvement. The Sunday papers continued the debate, with *The Sunday Times* awarding me the credit and commenting "operating with military precision, Veitch moved his troops under the radar".

Another story appeared in print a week or so later. In the Post, Jim Cremin wrote a very entertaining piece about the gamble, which praised my efforts and criticised those of the on-course bookmakers for failing to ignore the internet betting and instead devise their own price, an unlikely prospect in my experience. I was branded 'Bookmakers' public enemy No. 1'.

The only drawback to the article was the suggestion that we had somehow misplayed our hand, due to my agents asking for bets that were too large and setting the alarm bells ringing. Jim had been misled by his bookmaking contacts here. Bets were placed in all shapes and sizes at 100-1. There were indeed a few sizeable ones, but I might add that not every large bet was refused and it only needed the odd one to slip through the net for a huge profit. In fact, we needed the alarm bells to ring once we had taken our share of 100-1. This allowed the price to contract to a level where bookmakers and internet players were prepared to lay bigger bets at lower odds.

In my view, only one thing could have improved the execution of the business, and it was too much to expect. I have dreams in which a horse gets loose before the start of this race and causes a ten-minute delay. Had this happened, the betting exchanges would have allowed me to place further huge sums on Exponential. The odds would have continued to shorten and I would have filled up at every price, as more and more layers convinced themselves that the gamble had now gone to a silly price and needed to be opposed. The starting price was 8-1, but if luck had given me more time it would have been

2-1 and the extra winnings would have been well into six figures. Sadly, a ten-minute delay was too much to hope for.

My refusal to go public was to have one irritating consequence. A couple of years later, John McCracken, an infamous punter who had been warned off the racecourses for an indefinite period for associating with jockeys, sent out mailshots claiming to be the man behind the gamble. Racing has rightly done its best to rid itself of this character and fortunately no-one took the mailshot seriously, but it was annoying nonetheless. If even one person confused me with an individual like that then it would be one person too many.

The only disappointment to emerge from Nottingham was Exponential's future career. Stuart thought he was a Listed horse in the making, but sadly he never achieved form that was even close to that level. He suffered problem after problem as a three-year-old and went rapidly downhill, but he had done his job at two and owed us nothing. He was eventually bought at the sales by Milton Bradley, a trainer who does famously well with cast-offs from other yards. Exponential did win a little race for him in modest grade but that was the limit of his success, as even Bradley could not persuade him to repeat that victory.

But, on the afternoon that mattered most, Exponential did not let me down. That was my best-ever day's business. The money I won wasn't the most I've collected in one hit and, by 2004, a win of that size didn't have anything like the impact of some touches in my comeback year. But for sheer execution, I feel it was the one bet where I got everything right. We went to war with a horse who was regarded as nailed on by an ultra-shrewd trainer. The coup was organised down to the finest detail, so that he was still completely ignored at 100-1 a few minutes before the off. If I had my time again I honestly wouldn't do anything differently.

PART THREE
ON THE INSIDE

CHAPTER 21

CALM BEFORE
THE STORM

FRIDAY, July 30, 2004 was by no means an average day for my operation. Turnover was sky high and the results were not typical either, but describing in detail one of my busiest days will probably reveal more than a report of a standard day. As I've said, it is only by looking back a number of years that I am able to reveal the full day's activities. Detailing more recent trading would provide too many clues that would allow bookmakers to trace my future business.

It was the fourth day of five at Glorious Goodwood. I would travel to the course in the late morning and stay there until after racing on the Saturday. The previous three days had been spent in the office. Financially, I was slightly in front, but there had been no huge wagers as yet.

The alarm in my London flat went off at 8am. During the summer I wake up at the same time nearly every morning. That time is later than in previous years, ensuring that the occasional late night is not too disruptive to my sleep patterns. Occasionally, after a very late Saturday night, I'll have a Sunday morning lie-in, although I'll rouse myself to switch my phone on at 9.45 as one of my trainers might be trying to contact me about declaring a horse before the 10am deadline. My sleep patterns change completely when the winter break arrives. As nightlife in the UK has moved to more continental hours, especially in London, I often keep much later hours. I'm careful to check any horse declarations in advance, as I simply sleep until my body tells me to wake.

I ate breakfast straight after waking. I have quite a high metabo-lism, so my blood sugar falls overnight, causing me to wake hungry. Taking any sort of financial decision before eating would be unwise, as my typically positive mood is reversed until some food wakes up my system, so I settled down to read the *Racing Post* over a bowl of cereal. Having read the news, I reviewed the previous day's results. The major draw biases still in place in 2004 were already having an impact at Goodwood, but the situation was far from static. Continued watering through the week, combined with movement of the run-ning rails, made for a complex situation. Having finished the paper and breakfast, I headed for the shower and got dressed for the races.

Just after 8.30, I was back at my desk to review my shortlist of horses for Friday, prepared the night before. A full list had been scanned, containing more than 300 horses I'd made notes on during the preceding months. Some were negative, some were positive, but for all there was some reason to expect that the betting market might misread their chances on subsequent runs.

Eighteen 'list horses' were running that day, of which ten had been eliminated the day before. In most cases, detailed study showed that they might not be good enough, even allowing for any anticipated improvement. Others were taken out as their race was unsuitable. In the case of positive notes, there was often a nuance that I believed to be hiding a horse's true potential. Softer ground might have been needed, or maybe a longer distance, or perhaps a track more in keeping with the horse's characteristics. If a positive list horse was not facing optimum conditions I would ignore it and wait for a more suitable contest.

Negative list horses needed to feature prominently in the betting in their chosen race. If there was to be value in opposing them, then interest would be very limited if they were available at a double-fig-ure price. My negative choices would, as always, have been a major surprise to most racing experts. Compiling lists of underachieving or lazy horses was pointless, as these would be ruthlessly opposed in the betting market, so the negatives were mostly horses who seemed to have excelled on their latest starts but who I had judged to be overrated. A typical example might be a horse who had won by four lengths, with the jockey taking it easy close home. I might have decided that the manner of victory was less impressive than the experts believed, or that the race was substandard, particularly if this was not reported elsewhere.

The shortlist of eight needed further analysis. I analysed form lines on the computer while comparing a range of time- and form-based ratings in each of the chosen races. The ratings provided a guide but the detailed form study was far more important. All ratings are based on assumption, the estimates that either manual or computerised compilers make at the time they are produced. I needed to rework the form of the main contenders in each race, checking the assumptions against the latest form evidence. A race would look significantly weaker or stronger after the protagonists had raced again. Such study would continue many levels deep. Not only would the recent races of contenders be reworked, but the previous outings of the runners in *those* races would be reworked as well. A race that had occurred a month earlier would be reworked in both directions, reassessing the contenders in terms of the latest evidence about their past and future performances.

My hard drives had the last five years of racing fully indexed, so I could flick up the video of any race in seconds. A contender for the day, or a horse who had provided a key formline by racing again, would be watched in detail to see if its bare form looked in any way misleading. By 9.15, my shortlist had been narrowed down to five main contenders, plus a key note about the draw.

All For Laura (Nottingham 6.20) came from a race at Newmarket in early June that I'd been keen to oppose. I hadn't been taken with her performance on that debut and felt she might be a false price next time.

Blue Dakota (Goodwood 3.50) was noted as one to oppose if trying six furlongs. He'd scrambled home over five furlongs at Ascot and I'd been surprised to read afterwards that a step up in trip was likely.

Inter Vision (Thirsk 4.45) was noted after two runs on easier ground after a promising effort at Thirsk. Very well treated on a rating of 79.

Lucky Spin (Goodwood 2.40) wasn't as impressive as many had thought when winning a moderate Listed event at Warwick on her previous start and listed as one to oppose.

Nordwind (Nottingham 7.20) as usual, I'd seen little of the all-weather racing, but had happened to see Nordwind rout a field of maidens at Lingfield a fortnight earlier. He'd been seriously impressive, much more than the pundits seemed to believe. I felt they had underestimated the extent to which a step up in distance would bring enormous improvement.

DRAW: 3.15 High+++, 5.35 extremes?? The William Hill Mile at 3.15 saw a huge advantage for those drawn high. They would race towards the inside on ground that was both faster and less damaged by recent racing. The draw on the sprint course was more complex, but I suspected that the ground was quicker on the two flanks. A large field at 4.25 would provide a key indicator as to which flank was favoured and by how much.

I was in the middle of a thunderstorm, a time when my reading of the form is working particularly well and I take advantage by increasing both the size and quantity of my investments. On a day with plenty of interest, I had to make some major decisions, and needed to get some of the races sorted early. That way I wouldn't have too many balls to juggle once I left for the track, so the next hour was spent making some betting decisions and discussing them with my trading manager Geoffrey Pooley.

Lucky Spin had to be opposed in the Oak Tree Stakes at 2.40, and I fancied the chances of Chic, trained by Sir Michael Stoute. She'd been travelling exceptionally well when clipping the heels of another runner in a strong race at Ascot the time before. I didn't feel I had a huge edge, however, as the form was well exposed, so I gave Geoffrey a bet of £3,000. I only wanted to play at the best of the prices available.

In the 3.15, I'd placed a relatively small ante-post bet on Ancient World on Wednesday. I'd been asked to place a bet for a well-connected source and had followed the money in the light of his draw, 20 of 22, which was a huge advantage. I'd placed bets at 25-1, 20-1 and 16-1, totalling £1,360 each-way. Many others followed in the gamble as word spread of some impressive home gallops, and he was to start 9-2 favourite on the day. In fact, he wasn't a strong fancy of mine. The draw, combined with his long odds, had made a small bet hard to resist despite my reservations about his form. At the morning prices I favoured Sawwaah and Unshakable, in stalls 22 and 21, so I gave Geoffrey instructions to place £5,000 each-way on each during the morning.

Although a thunderstorm does enormous damage to our betting accounts, Geoffrey and The Robot had worked hard to ensure they had access to many new betting outlets, as they needed to arrange for bets to be placed on accounts that were not 'marked' by previous warm business. Providing they used unmarked accounts, placing large bets on a 22-runner handicap at Glorious Goodwood would not be too difficult.

Moving on to Blue Dakota in the 3.50, I fielded against him with a bet of £4,000 on Stetchworth Prince. I'd also opposed Blue Dakota at Ascot, figuring that the stiff uphill finish would not suit him, and his narrow victory had proved expensive. I was more cautious this time, but Stetchworth Prince's debut win at Newmarket had been boosted when the runner-up Army Of Angels had won two days earlier in a fast time.

Nordwind looked the strongest bet of the day at Nottingham, as I was quite confident that he could defy a handicap rating of 75. The main question was how to time the bet, and we felt that early afternoon would be the time to strike. Bookmakers would be fielding huge turnover for Goodwood and it would be much easier to hide our business among this level of activity; it was a good day to hide bad news for the bookmakers.

With a strong hand of new outlets, Geoffrey was confident of being able to place my stake of £20,000. He would typically try to place an additional 25 per cent for himself in such circumstances. In particularly strong markets, I might describe a bet as '40 per cent okay', meaning that I authorised him to place a stake of up to 40 per cent of my bet for himself. Although the bet would not be placed for many hours, it suited me to clear as many items off my list as possible. There was always the option to change the bet if there was a development in the meantime, but at this stage I could assume that the bet would be placed during the afternoon and I'd receive a phone call or text message confirming my return.

With morning betting dealt with, I had just over an hour to start making inroads into the video study for the previous day. I had to review the meetings at Goodwood, Carlisle, Epsom and Musselburgh. There was no hope of finishing in that time, but it was vital to use windows of time when they became available. The next opportunity to study the tapes would be Sunday, and it would be a huge burden to finish three full days at one session.

The problem is one of maintaining a very high level of sustained effort. It's possible to work without a break for 12, 14 or 16 hours, but scientific tests have proven that the quality of mental activity deteriorates quite rapidly after periods of immense concentration. A novice helicopter pilot is rarely allowed to fly for more than 30 minutes in the first few lessons – their performance usually drops quite rapidly after this time as the level of concentration takes its toll.

Watching race videos to a high standard is immensely tiring. You are watching 15 different stories unfold at the same time, so there is never a period when the eyes and mind can coast for a few seconds. The mind is constantly darting from horse to horse looking for something noteworthy. Of course, it would be easy to relax and simply let the race unfold, waiting for a performance to stand out, but this is not what is required. The purpose of watching a race is not to seek a performance that is 'impressive' or 'unimpressive'. Instead, a horse who is 'underestimated' or 'overestimated' is needed. Finding a performance that the experts have misunderstood is a hugely exacting process.

For each runner, it is necessary to watch both horse and jockey with great care. Scrutiny of the jockey will show the extent to which a runner is being restrained or urged forward. This can be fairly easy to spot, but in some cases the style of the rider or a restricted view will make it more difficult. Occasionally, I may conclude that the jockey is concealing his true level of effort by performing arm movements purely for show, with little effect on the horse. This is usually spotted by watching the precise movement of the hands and reins. The hands will typically move significantly less in a forward and back direction and, crucially, the reins will stay tight. When this lack of communication between rider and horse is accompanied by shaking of the elbows, my suspicions will be aroused. Air shots with the whip are a rather less subtle tactic, seen more rarely these days.

Watching the horse itself provides vital clues. The eye needs to be trained to spot horses who are suited or unsuited by the track or prevailing going. The pundits will focus on the more obvious clues, aware that a horse with a flowing stride will often perform well on fast ground, whereas a more awkward stride with plenty of bend in the knee will suit soft ground. These are acceptable rules of thumb, but as with betting as a whole, it is often more valuable to spot those occasions when the simple rule is wrong. Each horse is also watched in terms of in which sections of the race it is working hardest, and whether that was a wise use of energy at that point in the race. Once again, I'm looking for the underrated performance, not just one that is overtly promising.

As usual, The Robot watched the races with me. Although I was relying mainly on my own assessments, having a second party to bounce ideas off was an advantage. A second pair of eyes to suggest "what about the one in blue, out the back, he's taking it fairly easy on that one isn't he?" helped ensure that I missed as little as possible. After an hour, we'd completed only the meetings at Goodwood and Carlisle, and I'd made notes to keep an eye on seven horses. Three more would be added on Sunday when I studied the second half of the day. The total of ten was a little below average for a busy racing day. My notes show that Friday provided a massive contrast, with 26 horses recorded for further scrutiny when they reappeared.

I now had 15 minutes to finish getting ready for the races. I would carry only the notes and printouts I needed. Everything else, including my travel bag and clothes, was packed and ready to go in my Mercedes. The Robot's assistant Gareth was ready to drive down to The Spread Eagle Hotel at Midhurst, along with Greg, my computer programmer. They would jointly set up a remote office in my hotel room.

Just before 11.30am, I headed for the door. Penny, my personal assistant, had made all the arrangements regarding my travel and she handed me the helicopter bag. For each journey this contains printouts of maps and aerial photos for the pilot, as well as precise landing instructions. Landings at Goodwood are contracted out to a specialist company, with whom booking had to be made in advance. They supply a precise route into the racecourse, as well as a radio service to co-ordinate the arrival of the various machines. The bag also contained my satellite phone, which looks like a throwback to the first generation of mobile phones, being about eight inches long and three inches wide and deep. It doesn't look very cool.

A car had been booked to take me to Battersea Heliport, a journey that takes between 20 and 30 minutes, depending on traffic. This was a brief chance to relax, fitting a couple of social calls into the steady stream of racing-related ones. On the business front, some information was coming in about the day's runners, although nothing that changed my betting plans. I also used the time to discuss news with a couple of my trainers. There were a few runners due the following week and we needed to choose between races, as well as selecting a jockey.

Just before midday, I arrived at Battersea's tiny terminal. My machine, G-VEIT, was already on one of the landing spaces outside. Penny had booked the departure to be 'rotors running', which meant that the pilot did not shut down the machine and I could be away in seconds, so I was led straight out by Leon, a regular face at the heliport. Arrangements were normally fairly easy at Battersea, unless a general election was imminent, in which case the party leaders and their security arrangements tended to get in the way.

I sat in the front passenger seat next to my regular pilot Julian Vacher, who radioed for permission to leave immediately. For safety reasons, as a single-engine helicopter, we were only allowed to fly out of London along the Thames, so we headed west along the river for a couple of minutes before turning south for Goodwood. With favourable weather conditions, we made it to the racecourse in around 25 minutes, a huge time saving over a car journey, particularly with raceday traffic to contend with. As the distance was relatively short, Julian would return the helicopter to its base near London, allowing him to go home and return the following day. On longer journeys, the pilot stays overnight and leaves the helicopter at a nearby airfield.

At the track, I had an hour and a half before racing to finalise plans. Some friends had already arrived and secured a table on the lawn as a base. We had a chat and I took a few more calls, most importantly to update on morning business with Geoffrey. In a strong market, everything had gone to plan, with the exception of Chic, where my firm minimum price instruction had resulted in a slightly reduced return of £2,510. The Nordwind business would start a little later.

I made a couple of calls regarding the 6.20 at Nottingham. I was keen to oppose All For Laura and checked reports about the unraced Stoute filly Regina. Word reached me that she was not fully wound up, but might be ready to win first time. Not a strong positive, but a source I respected felt she would be good value. There was very hot money in the same race for Neverletmego, trained by Geoff Wragg, with talk of her being a strong favourite. She was the first foal out of the Group 1-winning sprinter Cassandra Go, which would further shorten her price but raised a question in my mind. Cassandra Go had not shown quality form until she was four and her high-quality brother Verglas had also been beaten on his debut. With a family that suggested gradual improvement, I was happy to oppose her with a small bet on Regina, and left Geoffrey a stake of £4,000 to be placed nearer the time.

At the same time, I received word from a profitable source for Akilana in the 7.25 at Galway. I had no time to study the Irish form but the past record of the source led me to place a bet of £1,500, obtaining prices of around 3-1 in a thin market. The final word during lunchtime came from the Mick Easterby camp. New Wish, in the 7.50 at Nottingham, had been laid out for the race and I was invited to place a lumpy bet for connections. A stake of £5,300 was required, and connections were happy to be guided by my views as to when the business should be placed. I put Geoffrey in charge of watching the betting with care. I suspected that a move during the afternoon would be wise, although the hot nature of the business would make it unwise to use the freshest accounts. Instead, we'd use a wide team of agents, splitting the business into a multitude of smaller amounts. New Wish had plummeted in the ratings over the previous season, down from 90 to 66. Although it was hard to be certain how much ability he retained, it was still impossible to resist backing him, given the knowledge that he was fit and fancied on his reappearance. I decided on a stake of £8,000 and would await news of the market.

The stage was set for a big afternoon, an afternoon that combined the delights of spending a beautiful summer afternoon with friends and of feverish betting turnover during a purple patch. I didn't have many more decisions to take in the early part of the afternoon so I took it easy on the lawn, bantering with friends between races. There would be more decisions later on, but for an hour or two I could relax.

CHAPTER 22

HECTIC HOURS
OF PUNTING

THE first race went by without a financial involvement, and in the second race, my small bet on Chic was a loser. She was perhaps set too much to do before finishing third and was to win in slightly stronger company next time. I was correct to oppose Lucky Spin, who actually finished last, but made no profit from her defeat.

Race three, the William Hill Mile, featured Sawwaah, Unshakable and my small ante-post bet on Ancient World. As usual, I moved from the lawn to view the race on a TV screen in the main stand. I've never had much interest in watching races live. In my view, the sight of owners and trainers watching races with binoculars is a throwback to a bygone age. A far greater understanding of a race can be obtained by carefully watching the televised coverage.

The race did not go as planned, with a steady pace not suiting either of my main fancies. With additional trouble in running, both failed to fire, and in the closing stages I had only Ancient World running for me. He managed to prevail by a length and a quarter, and I felt a little fortunate to have made a profit on the race. He hadn't appealed to me at the raceday prices and it was only the combination of a strong whisper and an enticing ante-post price that had caused me to step in. On a point of professional pride, I much prefer winners that come from my own judgement.

In the Richmond Stakes at 3.50, Stetchworth Prince ran just a fair race in finishing fourth behind Montgomery's Arch. My decision to oppose Blue Dakota (sixth) was correct, but I failed to instruct Geoffrey to lay him, despite a price of only 9-4. It was time for a rare piece of post-race self-criticism, a habit I limit to an absolute minimum.

After a race, a punter's natural tendency is to regard winning bets as 'good decisions' and losing bets as 'bad decisions'. From a financial point of view, this is true by definition, but in terms of assessing the quality of the thinking, this is frequently not the case. My decision to have a bet is based on my subjective judgement as to whether the odds on offer over- or underestimate a horse's chance of winning. As I am analysing a collection of horses running across a field, this pre-race judgement will frequently not be borne out by the result. This doesn't mean that the pre-race analysis was poor, it usually just means that the pre-race analysis failed to predict the correct result. A mental reproach at this point creates the danger of affecting future decisions by focusing the mind on avoiding a mythical 'mistake'.

There are only two occasions where immediate self-criticism after a race is justified. Firstly, when the race reveals that something clear has been missed from the analysis. Backing a horse who normally wears blinkers without spotting that the headgear has been omitted would be an example. Careful analysis should prevent this type of mistake, but they happen occasionally. The only other justification for criticism occurs on the rare occasion when I realise my business totally failed to reflect a very strong opinion that I held before the race. This second reason was the case in point with Blue Dakota. I had viewed a victory for the favourite as most unlikely and should have taken a strong position as a layer. Having lost on the same horse at Ascot, I had been too cautious. Over a full extra furlong, the circumstances were entirely different and I should have capitalised. A risk of, say, £20,000 was appropriate to my opinion, including laying Blue Dakota in the place market, which would also have collected. With Blue Dakota long odds-on for a place, a profit in excess of £10,000 would have resulted.

Such after-race criticism should be rare, occurring only in those circumstances where there is absolutely no doubt that I had drawn a very strong conclusion before the race and failed to act on this. The far more common occurrence – seeing a vague opinion borne out by the result – needs to be ignored. Vague opinions will often turn out to be correct, but are not reasons to trade.

Now it was time to move on. The next decision must be taken without any negative emotion from a bad result. This is perhaps the most difficult skill that a punter has to master. Most serious punters report that their worst decisions are taken in the second half of a trading day that started badly, after frustration got the better of them. Apart from sheer determination, I use a change of subject at this point to assist the mind in moving on calmly. So, despite being in the middle of one of the busiest meetings of the year, I found a quiet spot to make a social call. I spent five minutes just chatting on the phone about something completely unrelated. It's a simple technique but it tends to work, avoiding the need for the mind to spin round in frustration.

The next race at Goodwood was the 4.25, a 21-runner sprint handicap. I didn't have any strong view of the likely winner here, but felt there was a strong chance that the race would provide much greater clarity regarding any draw bias. Although the week had started on good ground, a sunny few days had made it necessary to add plenty of water to prevent the ground becoming too firm. In 2004, watering techniques made it likely that this would produce a substantial bias.

Sure enough, the result provided the clue I was looking for. The race showed a substantial bias to those racing close to the stands' rail, with a position very close to the rail a big advantage. In a 21-runner field, four of the first five home were drawn between 1 and 6. Not only that, those four horses were a fairly motley bunch, including the extremely moderate 66-1 shot Icenaslice. It was possible that the extreme far rail of the track would prove equally fast, as this had not been tested in the 4.25. The races on the round track had suggested that the far rail was quicker than the centre of the course.

That meant I needed to go to war in the 5.35, a 26-runner handicap over six furlongs. I was convinced that the race would be won by a horse racing on one of the extremities, with the stands' side slightly more likely. The huge bonus was that I had reviewed the race in the morning. Although nothing had made the shortlist, I still had an opinion. Of my three main fancies, two were drawn close to the stands' rail: High Ridge (4) and Merlin's Dancer (5). The other, Albashoosh, was drawn closest of all to the far rail (26). In addition, Merlin's Dancer was a front-runner who would have every chance to steal the favoured stands' rail. It seemed possible that the prices would contract if the draw bias became clear to others, so I gave Geoffrey my order straight away. The early-price market was still open and would be very strong in the middle of the meeting. I wanted £5,000 each-way Merlin's Dancer, £4,000 each-way Albashoosh and £3,000 each-way High Ridge.

Meanwhile, I had to take care of business at Thirsk, where Inter Vision was running in the 4.45. I recruited help from some other agents and spread a stake of £5,000, along with a £1,000 saver on outsider Drury Lane. Returns came back almost full at £4,830 and £950. Inter Vision ran the better of the pair, beaten just over a length in fourth, but not good enough. Drury Lane was last. Five minutes later, Geoffrey was back with returns for the 5.35. He'd obtained £4,850 each-way Merlin's Dancer, £4,000 each-way Albashoosh and £2,800 each-way High Ridge – close enough to the full totals.

As I headed towards the owners' and trainers' bar to watch the 5.00 I bumped into David Nicholls, who was fielding an amazing 11 of the 26 runners in the 5.35. I said hello, wished him good luck with his army, and told him that I thought the ground was fastest right on the stands' rail. I suggested Merlin's Dancer would be very hard to catch if he grabbed the rail as early as he was allowed to. I made a point of not asking David which he fancied. Trainers are often inundated with people asking their opinion at the races, and I wanted it to be clear that my thinking was genuine, rather than an excuse to extract information. My attitude was also a lot more restrained than when I spoke to David about Pepperdine on the same day five years earlier. He thanked me before rushing off, no doubt to supervise the collection of 11 saddles from the weighing room.

Just before 5.35, I took up a position in front of a TV screen close to the exit. Gareth would be waiting outside and missing the traffic would be a huge benefit. In terms of the betting, I was a little surprised that my fancies had not shortened as much as expected. High Ridge had shortened into 9-1, having been 16-1, but Merlin's Dancer, backed at prices between 10-1 and 12-1, returned at 10-1. Albashoosh had actually drifted from the price we had taken.

Despite the news from the betting ring, the race itself panned out marvellously. Merlin's Dancer grabbed the rail as I hoped and made all, followed home by High Ridge. Albashoosh ran well on the far side to finish fourth, so that all three bets were in profit. Business rarely works out so well. An average day had suddenly become a very good one, with a profit of nearly £70,000 on Merlin's Dancer alone. In the middle of the thunderstorm, there is no time to dwell on how the profit or loss moves from race to race. Unless I have made a clear-cut mistake, such as Blue Dakota, it pays to move on immediately. Even basking in the winners is not wise, as it makes it harder to move on after a loser if the brain is not in the habit of doing so.

On the way out I bumped into David again, strutting in the opposite direction towards the winner's enclosure. This was becoming a habit. We quickly shook hands, simultaneously saying 'well done' before heading in our respective directions. Within a couple of minutes I was in the Mercedes, being driven by Gareth back to the Spread Eagle. During the afternoon, Gareth and Greg had set everything up in the room. Greg dealt with the IT side, principally ensuring that the video database was operational using the latest portable hard disk drives we had bought. These had been updated with all the latest video files from the server at home.

Gareth's main task had been to organise my printouts, so that I was able to study the cards as quickly as possible on my return. I had one sheet containing the overnight runners for each meeting and then four further sets of printouts, containing a wide variety of ratings for the next day. These were placed on the desk next to my books of video notes. Finally, he had supplied me with a list of my noted horses that were declared to race on Saturday. He dropped me at the hotel at 6pm and headed home with Greg. Gareth would be returning alone at the end of my stay to retrieve the travelling office and return it to London.

During the journey, I had received an update on business for Nottingham. As planned, Geoffrey had placed most of the business during the action at Goodwood. The two largest bets had been placed with contrasting methods. A wide variety of agents had placed the New Wish business for the Easterby camp, and my return came to the curious total of £8,097.80, a fraction over my request. Nordwind, a less 'warm-looking' bet, had been placed with much more subtlety on unmarked accounts, with a full return of £20,000. The only remaining bet, on Regina, was to be placed shortly before the 6.20 race.

It was time for some exercise. I've always found that a spell in the gym makes me much more able to focus and make accurate decisions over the following 24 hours. There wasn't time for a full workout but I lifted some weights and did some cardiovascular work, finishing just inside the hour, during which time I received a text to report that Regina had been beaten. Victory had gone to All For Laura, the horse

I had aimed to oppose. She had clearly improved dramatically for her first run.

There were a couple of hours before dinner. Friends were staying in the same hotel and we were due to meet in the bar at 9pm. Goodwood is by far the quietest of the major meetings in terms of nightlife, so we were just having dinner at the hotel. I settled down to work on my long list of noted runners for the following day. The aim was to eliminate at least half of them, as I had done the previous evening. Twenty-five of Saturday's runners had been noted on my list and I set to work studying the races. The portable hard drives worked a treat; I could flick up race videos just as quickly as I did in the office. As I worked, I set my phone alarm for 7.19 and then 7.49, as reminders to phone for commentaries at Nottingham. On past visits to Midhurst I'd wandered round to the local betting shop once or twice, but I had enough work to do. Geoffrey, The Robot and I had long used the adage 'they don't run any faster when you watch them'. Anyway, I'd be watching the races in full detail when working through the videos.

Nordwind scraped home to land the biggest single bet of the day in the 7.20. The commentator never sounded confident and the victory was only a head. He would need to step up another two furlongs before winning again. New Wish failed to fire in the 7.50 and proved a disappointment, as did my small bet on Akilana (fourth) at Galway. With all the results in, I interrupted my form study to balance the day's figures.

Goodwood	2.40	Chic £2,510	-£2,510
Goodwood	3.15	Sawwaah £5,000 e/w	-£10,000
Goodwood	3.15	Unshakable £5,000 e/w	-£10,000
Goodwood	3.15	Ancient World £1,360 e/w	+£35,730 *ante-post*
Goodwood	3.50	Stetchworth Prince £4,000	-£4,000.00

Thirsk	4.45	Inter Vision £4,830	-£4,830
Thirsk	4.45	Drury Lane £950	-£950
Goodwood	5.35	Albashoosh £4,000 e/w	+£5,118.75
Goodwood	5.35	High Ridge £2,800 e/w	+£5,600
Goodwood	5.35	Merlin's Dancer £4,850 e/w	+£69,500
Nottingham	6.20	Regina £3,950	-£3,950
Nottingham	7.20	Nordwind £20,000	+£64,250
Galway	7.25	Akilana £1,500	-£1,500
Nottingham	7.50	New Wish £8,097.80	-£8,097.80

Turnover of £91,857.80 produced a profit of £134,360.95. A pleasing day, but again I didn't allow myself time to reflect on the results.

By 9pm, I had reduced the shortlist from 25 to 11. My early conclusions were that Fong's Thong was very likely to win the 2.30 at Goodwood on Saturday, but all would depend on the price as he was sure to be popular (he won at 6-4). The main interest would be the six-furlong Stewards' Cup, where I was extremely confident that the outside flanks would again dominate. The draw biases allowed me to make hay in these situations and I was sure to be involved (Pivotal Point would win from stall 1).

With the day's work done, I headed down to dinner. As typifies evenings at Goodwood, it was a fairly relaxed affair, and I managed to steer most of the conversation away from racing as I was ready for a break. Towards the end of dinner I received a text message urging me to head into London to go clubbing. The offer was tempting, but I knew there were major battles to fight on Stewards' Cup day and declined. I'm not known for being in bed too early, but I made it by half past midnight. It was midway through the summer and my batteries would need plenty of recharging if I was to make it through to the autumn . . .

CHAPTER 23
TIME OFF

IN A FULL working year, I now expect to do about 180 days' work, including trips away from the office to Ascot, Goodwood and York. The middle of the summer is always the hardest period of the year, with non-stop racing every day and almost every evening, but over time I've been able to delegate every part of my work except for the key winner-finding decisions, and by employing a computer programmer I've been able to automate much of the research work and produce reports to speed up my manual scrutiny. Everything is aimed at getting my work done as efficiently as possible, and matters that don't need my studied attention, like travel arrangements or the servicing of a car, are taken care of by my two personal assistants.

I spend most of my time at my house in the country. Past experiences make me a little cautious about these matters, so I won't publish its location, although it's not a secret among those who know me well. I've always thought moving house every couple of years is a waste of time, so I decided to get the job done once and for all by finding a place I was unlikely to outgrow. I've renovated the house to make guests very welcome; the middle of summer is still very hectic so it makes it much easier for friends to see me at that time of the year.

Mindful of past experiences, security is a top priority. I've invested in the widest possible range of high-level security systems for the house and grounds. Just to be on the safe side, I've chosen not to invest in expensive paintings or objects and don't keep cash or valuables at home either. I've served my time as a victim of crime and I'm confident that I would now be the most foolish choice in England for another criminal to select as a target. The renovation activity caused considerable interest locally. Lucy, one of my personal assistants, has been amusing herself by telling inquisitive taxi drivers and the like that my wealth came from bringing Sudoku to Britain.

Although I still have a couple of fast cars, my helicopter has provided me with the greatest travelling pleasure over the last five years. I had mine designed in my racing colours of dark blue and light brown. Horseracing is perhaps the best occupation in which to use a helicopter, as business meetings involve racecourses that are perfect for landing spots and the helicopter can travel from where it's stored to collect me from my lawn.

I made copious research into the safety of various models and the factors that have led to helicopter crashes before buying the machine. I know the risks and how to minimise them, and by travelling only with a professional pilot and in good daylight weather I can cut the potential for disaster to an absolute minimum. My knowledge didn't stop me getting all hot under the collar on one occasion, though, when my pilot for the day was ace flier Quentin Smith. 'Q' has flown helicopter expeditions all round the world and taken machines into the sky in conditions that I wouldn't consider sanctioning. Having previously reached the North Pole by helicopter, in 2003, he attempted to do the double by heading for the South Pole until he was forced to ditch into the Atlantic just short of the Antarctic. For him, a trip from London to York was as routine as brushing his teeth, so on the journey back he opted to forgo the normal 1,500ft below the clouds policy and head above the clouds to 5,000ft. This produced stunning views but his rate of ascent, which was much steeper than I was used to, left my palms clammy with sweat.

Another flying trip involved travelling to Sheriff Hutton in North Yorkshire, after which David Easterby and I had the onerous task of showing Miss England, Georgia Horsley, the pleasures of a day's racing at York. I've mentioned an encounter with a Miss Great Britain in my comeback year, but I didn't manage to get the treble up when another Miss England visited Newcastle races. I couldn't make it that day, but was available in the evening, only for David to earn himself the undisputed title of stupidest man in Britain when the girl's agent asked if he would be available in the evening if Miss England chose to stay overnight. "No, we always travel back from Newcastle the same day," had been his astonishing reply. Truly unbelievable. But you saved the £100 on a hotel room, didn't you mate, and I know how you like to hold on to every penny up in your neck of the woods.

Not every day at the races comes complete with a Miss England in tow but, during one memorable season, I was rarely seen at the races in the company of fewer than two models. After the early successes of Minivet and Great News, I considered widening my syndication of horses by advertising. I chose a syndicate name, Phoenix Racing, and decided to spend the summer examining the possibilities while promoting the name at the races, so for each racing visit it made sense to hire two models who would wear Phoenix Racing sashes to promote the brand. My friend Harvey Cyzer had left Henry Cecil's stable and now had plenty of time on his hands before launching a training career. He had the right connections, having previously worked for Next model agency in London, and for some reason he seemed much keener to come racing when he knew the models would be in attendance.

Before the Flat season began, we staged a marathon casting session in London to screen suitable girls for this taxing role. It was evidently a popular job, as we ended up with a conveyor belt of gorgeous girls arriving at five-minute intervals over two days. It was tough. Harvey and I had to suffer a stamina-sapping bout of sitting in comfortable armchairs in a casting studio, while a couple of hundred of the best-looking models in London came in one by one to chat to us. Now you're going to say that we simply chose the girls we fancied the most. Of course we did, we weren't stupid!

We travelled from major meeting to major meeting, each time taking two girls from our chosen list. What a summer that was. One of the agencies specialised in glamour models, so that for the York Dante meeting we had Page 3 girls Holly McGuire and Jakki Degg in our company for two days. Faced with the simple task of backing a 6-4 favourite that I quite fancied on the first day, I decided to let the girls put the money on. After some brief coaching, Harvey and I stood in the stands laughing as the fun unfolded. The whole betting ring watched with their eyes out on stalks as our two stunning models rushed around thrusting piles of £50 notes into bookmakers' hands. I could have struck a bet of £4,000 at 6-4 easily, but that wouldn't have offered half the entertainment.

The girls managed to get some of the money on at 13-8 with one bookmaker not known for laying big bets, or at least not to people who aren't Page 3 girls. This little bit of extra odds almost paid for the five per cent commission we'd agreed to give them if the horse won. They were pleased with their winnings, to say the least, and a great night out in York ensued. A couple of weeks later Alastair Down, from Channel 4 Racing, asked me to let him know if I would be bringing the same couple of girls to the next meeting. He said he needed to ensure that he packed the necessary heart pills for the trip if the viewing was going to be as pleasing.

Before anyone concludes that the whole situation sounds rather unromantic, there is a twist in the tale. The day after the casting, Harvey and I reviewed the videos taken of the shoot. One girl, Fay Lawson, really caught Harvey's eye. As soon as her segment had run, Harvey announced: "Fay Lawson, that's the girl I'm going to marry." Fay was duly invited to work for us more than once over the season and I'm pleased to report that Harvey has lived up to his word. By the end of the summer the pair had become inseparable, and Fay is now Mrs Cyzer and mother to their son, Rocky. In the end, I decided not to proceed with Phoenix Racing – but had an awful lot of fun making that decision.

Apart from that heady summer, I've kept a lower profile with my girlfriends, although one or two hit the headlines afterwards. One ex-girlfriend hit the front-page headlines in no uncertain style. A couple of years after we dated, she removed her jacket on a warm day at Royal Ascot to reveal a top that was almost entirely see-through. The sight of an attractive girl wearing such an outfit was too much for The Sun, and the next morning a huge photo of Charlotte appeared on the front page with an accompanying 'topless posh totty' story. Charlotte worked as an investment adviser for Barclays Bank, so I wouldn't have minded being a fly on the wall by the office water-cooler that day.

After embarking on a sabbatical at the end of 2006, I caught up with a whole host of things that I'd been too busy to enjoy in previous summers. I've always had plenty of spare time in my winter breaks, but for once I could devote time to summer activities such as tennis and barbecues. I also embarked on a series of courses including Indian cooking, massage, and an all-important lesson in making cocktails. It was fun taking time out and letting my brain tick a little less quickly than usual. As I was betting rarely during this period, I had plenty of time to think strategically about gambling, and pondered at length how best to allocate my time. Would it be possible, I wondered, to achieve the same level of profit from a lower workrate?

I also had more time to catch up with friends around the country without my phone buzzing as often as it does in a normal summer. I even had the chance to hatch a plot exposing those friends who had acquired nicknames over the years. I secretly sponsored a few races in their honour, with most of my victims unaware until the day that they would be presenting the trophies for races such as the George Swiers 'The Taxman' Nursery and the Simon Wood 'The Messenger' Handicap. The banter is quite competitive among my friends, so I'm sure my time will come.

I enjoy foreign holidays, although as my lifestyle has improved I haven't felt the need to leave home too often. I've had my share of trips to the Caribbean, Florida, Los Angeles and Dubai, and have made a few trips to Hong Kong with the family to visit my brother. Then there is a yearly trip to Las Vegas at the end of each Flat season with David Easterby and Colin Ferrett. We play poker, although I'm a tiny gambler at cards compared to horseracing. Poker is fun when played once a year but it's a little too similar to my day job to play on a regular basis.

The Vegas trip is tremendous fun. The Wynn is my favourite hotel in the world. Even if I had no interest in gambling I'd still not want to leave the hotel during the entire time I was there. David has calmed down his socialising in Britain in recent years, but when he is on holiday he is certainly keen not to let any bar end the night overstocked. One morning, Colin and I discovered that David was still at the poker tables and by now so drunk that he was unable to stand. Security sent for a wheelchair and I was asked to push him back to his room. I then had to force-feed him coffee and diet Coke for two hours to ensure he was fit to fly that afternoon. I've offered to buy a copy of the CCTV footage of the wheelchair incident but the Wynn has yet to co-operate.

The Vegas trip lasts four days, but another jaunt was even shorter. Having met a girl in London a few years ago and had one of the best nights out on record, I was dismayed when Caroline promptly announced that she was relocating to work in Australia for four years. I woke up a few weeks later, on New Year's Day, and decided that I wasn't going to be beaten, so I invited her out to dinner in Sydney, claiming to be there on a business trip. I thought that admitting in advance that I was travelling across the world just to take her out for dinner might seem a little forward. It proved to be another fantastic evening; I haven't been back a second time, but you never know . . .

CHAPTER 24

BRAIN SURGEONS AND MAD AXEMEN

I AM often asked what type of character is best suited to betting for a living. Strange as it may sound, the ideal choice is a split personality, as the processes of selection and trading have to be approached on an entirely different basis. The nearest description I have found is a combination of a brain surgeon and a mad axeman.

The selection process is carried out by the brain surgeon. He needs an entirely meticulous approach, as he researches every detail possible. He must be mentally consistent at all times. When he's done his part, the door is kicked open by the mad axeman. A willingness to trade aggressively, the ability not to care when a fortune is at stake on one day, and the force of mind to push on through all bookmaker resistance requires the mentality of a mad axeman. After the day is over, the brain surgeon takes over again, coolly assessing the results and planning the next day's betting after making adjustments for what has been learned.

The combination of the two sides of the character ensures that bets will be placed that can lose the value of a sports car in one race and the value of a house in a week without destroying the selection process. The ability to bring both sides to gambling in equal measure has brought me huge returns while never putting a large percentage of my capital at risk.

In the gambling world, there have been plenty of people who have mastered one side but not the other. There are brain surgeons who pick with meticulous detail but are not strong enough mentally

226

to bet in high stakes while keeping their selections consistent. Their bets stay within their comfort zone and their winnings are limited accordingly. Other brain surgeons fail because they are not willing to fight their way through the obstacles placed by the bookmakers. They simply accept that bookmakers are hostile to winners, and do not have the necessary mental energy or resolve to constantly seek out new ways to overcome this.

An example of the brain-surgeon mentality was provided in the film Casino. Sam 'Ace' Rothstein, played by Robert De Niro, depicts the story of the true-life gambler Frank 'Lefty' Rosenthal. In his role as a casino boss, De Niro's character is seen berating a chef for the inconsistency of his muffins. From now on, the chef must ensure a precisely equal number of blueberries in each muffin. Although Rosenthal was a shady character to say the least, his former life as a professional gambler had produced a 'brain surgeon' mind that had an obsessive desire to ensure that every detail was correct. He confirmed the muffin story word for word in a later interview.

Then there are the mad axemen. These are invariably people who can trade positions of any size and are willing to take the market on with continuous aggression. They usually come unstuck fairly quickly, but those who are more talented, luckier or very well-connected will last longer. But most will come unstuck in the end if they lack the disciplined, painstaking approach of a brain surgeon. Naturally, they will perform well enough when results are favourable, but they are at great risk when things go badly, as they will try to blast their way out of trouble without making the necessary adjustments to account for recent mistakes.

Before contemplating betting seriously, punters should assess their own mental strengths and weaknesses. If they lack the mad axeman touch but have the meticulous thoughts of a brain surgeon, then they must accept that they may become successful but not at a high level. If they have the wild instincts of a mad axeman but not the restraining caution of the surgeon, then they should expect to run out of money fairly often during their gambling career. It will be a roller-coaster ride.

One thing that can seriously affect mental processes is, of course, alcohol. During the racing season I'm extremely careful with my intake and even chose to abstain completely during a couple of my busiest summers. Now my workload is a little less frenetic, I'm inclined to allow myself the odd night out here and there. Fitness is another related subject. I rarely found the time to exercise in my first couple of years as a full-time punter, but this turned out to be a mistake. Regular extended days would leave me exhausted and far from effective in the second half of the day. Since I made exercise a priority, I've been able to focus throughout long days in the office. Long-term health is also a key consideration. A high percentage of professional gamblers I've known have suffered health problems during their career as long-term stress took its toll. Having seen the whole range of health issues, from heart problems to battles within the mind, I'm pleased to have come through some stressful early years in the best physical shape I could manage.

Although I like to think I have mastered both the brain surgeon and mad axeman sides, there are always periods when nothing seems to go right. In such periods it is possible to run up sizeable losses, however the size of my bets, although enormous by most standards, is always conservative relative to my capital. From the end of 1999, I've always been able to be almost certain that a losing run would not make deep inroads into my capital.

Of course, there are others who prefer a much more adventurous approach and will risk a far greater percentage of their capital in a short period. This will produce great rewards when results go well, but also create periods when capital is seriously depleted after a losing run. Had I adopted a riskier staking strategy over the years, I could have made total profits of at least double the actual figure by betting in huge sums on those occasions when the market is very strong, but one or two really bad years might have left me much worse off. Doubling my wealth would not have made me any happier, so I've chosen certainty over maximised profits.

Despite my careful approach, a long losing run is still immensely frustrating. The first months of 2005 provided my largest ever run of losses. A hugely successful 2004 had ended on a high, with profits of more than £200,000 in the final weeks after the Flat season ended in early November. I had been receiving some excellent guidance over jumps and following some consistently profitable business. During the winter, I don't balance my figures weekly, but I made a profit of £52,158.50 in the period November 28-December 12 and one of £92,992.24 from December 13-28.

Almost as soon as the new year turned, the wind blew in the opposite direction. The jumps business I received went through a terrible run and by the end of the Cheltenham Festival I had not had a winning period, running up the following losses.

29 December – 10 January:	-£26,569.00
11–24 January:	-£19,567.67
25 January – 6 February:	-£50,587.50
7–28 February:	-£11,774.40
1–19 March:	-£90,037.37

I'd incurred total losses of £198,535.94 in the first two and a half months of the year, nearly all my profit from the final two months of the previous year. The final period was by far the most painful, as I'd handled a succession of losing ante-post bets for Cheltenham. As the Flat season approached, I was extremely keen to redress the balance.

In a sense, it helped that the losses had come from following other business. My own selections are the main driver of profit each year and I take it far more personally if they fail over a lengthy period. Of course, all-weather racing had continued throughout the winter, but focusing on turf racing meant that the following weeks would allow my own business to take centre stage.

The turf season made a very slow start, with the Lincoln Handicap not taking place until April 2. During this first period I made some early profits and was starting to feel more comfortable. There were no major fireworks but I backed a steady stream of smaller winners.

19 March – 3 April: **+£43,784.64**

The next fortnight produced a steady run of losing bets. I normally balance up every week once the season starts, but was so frustrated after the first week that I chose to run a two-week account in the hope of avoiding writing up another loss. I traded fairly small in the very early weeks of the season, waiting for the form lines to gradually become clear. This proved the only wise decision I made. My early predictions were remarkably unsuccessful and the business I handled for others was similarly unprofitable, and I lost a six-figure sum over the two-week period, a sorry saga made all the more remarkable as only one single loss ran into five figures. Even that only cost me £11,000, when I'd done quite a lot of business on the John Porter Stakes at Newbury despite the race being outside my normal 5f-1m distance range. I'd been keen to oppose the winner, Day Flight, and had paid the penalty.

4–17 April: **-£109,128.05**

At this point, it was time to take a tough decision. I was finding the workload too intense. Having made huge profits in 2003 and 2004, I didn't feel the need to work quite so many hours during the summer.

I was still working very hard but took a little more time off and, as a result, the amount of business I was still handling for third parties was eating into my form study. My own analysis had led to the vast majority of the profits in the previous two years, so it was time to restrict business. I still maintained the most profitable sources, but had to request that others find other outlets for their business. This would lead to a considerable reduction in the number of bets each week, freeing up vital study time. The new strategy didn't bring immediate dividends, although at least there seemed to be a temporary respite from the losses, with a much smaller deficit the following week. There were no major results in either direction.

18–24 April: -£2,917.78

The next week was a terrible week. Increased amounts of study time failed to produce anything like the required returns, and my biggest loser was Lava Flow, who cost me £16,725. I'd fancied him strongly to win at Hamilton after he made a pleasing debut at Windsor, but he ran deplorably, presumably sustaining some sort of injury as he died without running again. Almost all my other selections failed to fire, with most not even running close. The reduced level of third-party business was also unprofitable and it all added up to a second six-figure losing period.

25 April – 1 May: -£113,130.85

The next week was a little better, if it is possible to categorise losing more than £30,000 as 'better'. Desperate times call for desperate measures. As mentioned in an earlier chapter, a huge punt on Strike Up The Band went astray in the Lily Agnes Stakes at Chester. After a hugely impressive performance at Pontefract, I was happy to unload on him despite a short price, risking £39,700 only to see him go down by a short head.

Elsewhere, there was some reason for comfort. Although I still hadn't landed a serious punt, a number of each-way selections hit the frame at decent prices, and in terms of how my fancies were actually running, I wasn't far away from making a profit. Still, I now found myself balancing my ninth losing period from ten that year, an unprecedented run of failure. I was now down by £412,006.84. Although this was only a tiny slice of my long-term profit, it was still a huge sum to lose in just over four months.

Dealing with a period of this gravity tests the mettle of the bravest gambler. When it happens to me, I try to stay focused and calm, because I know beyond doubt that a badly-needed return to form can only be achieved by a combination of steely determination and hard work. The negative effect on my state of mind starts to kick in when my losses over a short period approach £200,000. If I am down by £100,000 or even £150,000, I will accept that I have just had a few bad days. When you bet in the sort of sums that I do on a regular basis, you become used to losing £100,000 or so in a short period.

I become ever more determined, but for a period of time I will be a lot less happy in my work. I call this period 'serious mode'. Sometimes it feels as though I am trying to force myself up the steps of a long down escalator. I feel I am making the right moves but can't seem to make any headway. It's a serious business but, however bad things appear, it doesn't pay to change my approach. Past experience tells me that if I stick to my overall strategy I will end up on the right side of the business. Full release from serious mode doesn't come when the losses are reduced. I need all of them back and to be well into profit before I return to top form. I've probably hit serious mode on about five or six occasions since 1999 but the 2005 run was certainly a record.

2–8 May: -£32,078.86

The following week, results finally started to run in my favour. Although most of my profits come from longer-priced selections, it was a favourite that started the recovery process this time. Fort Dignity looked close to a certainty in a Listed race at Windsor on the Monday. I took 15-8, 7-4 and 13-8 in the morning betting and won £37,020 from a stake of £20,000 when he eased home by a neck. Three days later, a serious punt on Quito, who'd been found a surprisingly weak race at the York Dante meeting, netted me £66,500. The same day I won £40,712 when Ajigolo landed a Salisbury maiden, and suddenly I was back in full flow. A number of smaller winners helped me profit by £185,582.25 on the week, making a huge dent on the yearly losses. It was to be the start of a tremendous summer run.

I've already explained that a thunderstorm is a period in which I increase turnover dramatically if I am seeing the form clearly and making good profits. The mad axeman side of the personality becomes enhanced during these periods. At a time when my analysis is proving extremely successful, it is vital to be at my most aggressive with my trading. This will continue as long as my form holds up, which can produce a huge profit very quickly. In many years, the majority of my earnings comes from one period of just a few weeks. 2003, 2004 and 2005 produced the most striking returns, with more than a million pounds' profit from each thunderstorm. The 2005 storm was actually the smallest of the three, but after the nightmare start to the year, it was certainly the one I appreciated the most. The figures for my three most profitable thunderstorms are as follows:

2003

w/e 20 July to w/e 14 September – profit of **£1,318,012.50** in 9 weeks

2004

w/e 20 June to w/e 12 September – profit of **£1,630,408.34** in 13 weeks

2005

w/e 15 May to w/e 17 July – profit of **£1,212,309.39** in 10 weeks

CHAPTER 25

BOOKMAKERS AND SOME BETTING THEORY

HOW do I describe my occupation to strangers? I can count the number of players I really rate highly as professional punters on the fingers of one hand. This knowledge makes me a bit cautious about revealing the full extent of my betting activity when I meet someone socially for the first time. It is remarkable how many times they know someone who is also a professional punter. I am regaled with all manner of tall stories of their punting exploits.

If I am fortunate and this isn't the case, plenty of questions will usually follow. If I find the conversation particularly interesting, I will be open, breezy, chirpy, and reveal a bit more. I am even more careful when I am keen to move on through the type of queue you can encounter going through customs at an airport. Then I say that I am an investment strategist. This invariably does the trick by killing the conversation, because it makes my occupation sound so dull. Apologies to all investment strategists . . .

Most people outside racing are amazed that a considerable amount of my business time is devoted simply to trying to place my bet. At least I have this delegated to others these days. People are shocked to hear that under current legislation bookmakers can advertise prices and boast freely about their willingness to lay large bets, only to refuse point blank to take a single penny if they are too wary of the person placing the bet. People ask: "So they can quote you a price, refuse to take any bet at all, then change the odds?" The answer, shamefully, is yes. It is surely time to introduce minimum trading standards for bookmaking so that each firm is obliged to accept a minimum level of bet based on its liability.

Over the years, the bookmakers have become progressively more scared of my business. At times, this fear has bordered on obsession, with rumours in abundance about my activities. I've often been amazed by the amount of speculation about my supposed involvement on days when I haven't even had a bet. I suppose I should think it's flattering that bookmakers have frequently changed their procedures specifically to limit my winnings. This has happened many times. At first it occurred in lots of small ways. After we landed a major win, we'd hear about changes in trading policy from one firm or another.

For example, we'd discover that a bookmaker had halved the maximum liability that their traders could accept on any bet from an unproven client, or a trading manager had told his workforce to restrict all bets to a much smaller stake if they were from a list of stables with which I might have a connection. Avoiding Veitch business was invariably mentioned. In time, some of the rule changes became more radical, to the point that William Hill and Ladbrokes, two of the biggest betting companies in the world, would choose to completely reprogram their systems in an attempt to restrict my winnings.

Internet betting was their newest area of trading. The firms were able to alter the limits on individual accounts that turned over a profit. They could in effect shut them down, if they chose, by setting ridiculously low limits. However, it turned out that I had an awful lot of friends with internet accounts, and such retrospective action wasn't placing a sufficient limit on winnings. Ladbrokes and Hills then reprogrammed their systems so that every internet customer was restricted to much smaller bets on horses that came from stables they associated with me. For example, Ladbrokes would offer bets of £1,000 to unproven customers on all the runners at a meeting, except for those they associated with stables connected to me. Then the limit would be £100.

They would place these restrictions all day, every day, to try to cut down my winnings. As I've had horses in many stables, this restriction would apply to maybe ten per cent of runners on the Flat, depending on how many stables they associated me with that year. Such actions were naturally harmful to their business. Many of their other customers, who lose consistently, would fall foul of these same restrictions. They might place a few losing bets and then suddenly be offended to find that without explanation they were only allowed to place a much smaller bet. In an attempt to reduce my winnings, Ladbrokes and Hills were willing to alienate some of their day-to-day customers.

I imagine I am joint-holder of the record for the shortest-lived betting account of all time. When I first started betting, I did so in my own name, but before long restrictions and account closures started. When I phoned Sunderlands to request an account, the chap at the other end of the phone said that this was no problem, and asked for my name. When I told him, he immediately replied: "I'm sorry, we won't be able to help you." Yes turned to no in just five seconds. It became clear that betting in my own name was going to be pointless.

Even when the money's on, it's not always been possible to ensure payment. There have been two bookmakers who have simply refused to pay up, one small East Anglian independent who kept around £10,000 of my money and the infamous bookmaker run by Sonny Purcell. Purcell once appeared on Channel 4's The Morning Line as a fine example of an enterprising new bookmaker, only to go under leaving bets unpaid after trading with a distinct lack of caution. The Robot had an account with £12,000 in it that we never saw.

Let's now look at some betting strategy. Most of what is written about betting fails to address the fundamental principle of betting theory. This is that winning at betting requires the selection of an outcome whose chance is underestimated. It is simply a case of finding a bet where the odds are greater than the true chance of that event happening.

Many punters seem willing to debate endlessly the merits of value in betting, with those favouring a winner-finding strategy locking horns with those favouring an emphasis on seeking out value. I suppose one could say that the value side are correct, but the vagueness of the word causes unnecessary debate. 'Underestimated' is the correct word, because it is true by definition and also provides a continual reminder of the logical way to approach betting. There are further pointless debates about whether it is better to focus on shorter- or longer-priced selections. There is no right or wrong answer, as a 1-2 shot can be underestimated as much as a 50-1 chance. The betting market is now formed almost entirely by a consensus of expert opinion, with the price on the exchanges being the point at which a balance has been reached between layers and backers. If there was a clear advantage in backing horses at a certain price, the market would soon move to correct that.

So far, I've only pointed out the obvious. If a punter can't recognise that betting is, by definition, about finding something that is underestimated, then he really needs to give up very quickly. Where most gamblers go wrong is that they adopt selection methods that offer no prospect of finding underestimated horses. Let's look at some typical examples that will often be quoted as reasons for having a bet.

"He was really impressive last time out." "He'll love the soft ground today." "I've had a really good word for the newcomer trained by John Gosden."

These are the three most common criteria that punters use: comment on a recent run, comment about today's race, and information. Which of the three is a valid reason for considering a bet? None of them, of course. They all represent woolly thinking, and yet almost all racing analysis is conducted on this basis.

Each statement has ignored the fact that the market forms the odds with an obsessive interest in these sort of factors. The more impressive a horse was, or the more suited to the ground it will be, the shorter the odds will be. As the odds are a consensus of expert opinion, it is reasonable to expect that they will correctly assess how much shorter. Similarly, the market prices about an unraced horse of Gosden's will be based on the large amount of information that will circulate about that horse and will, on average, produce a price that reflects the consensus view of its chance.

Let's return to the three examples and see how they would need to be changed to produce something more relevant to finding an underestimated horse. Try these.

"I've analysed what has been said by the experts about his run last time out. I feel they have made a huge error in the way they've described his performance. He was far, far more impressive than the consensus of expert opinion believed."

"The market's view of how effective he'll be on today's ground is entirely incorrect. It is presumed that he doesn't like soft ground, but his stable was badly out of form when he tried soft in the spring and, watching the way he gallops, I'm fairly confident it will really suit him."

"I've had a good word for the newcomer of John Gosden's. When I've had information from this source, it has tended to involve horses who have not been heavily backed, yet they have a consistent record of running well and almost always perform better than their odds would suggest."

You'll see how each quote has been changed from looking for a positive factor to an underestimated factor. A punter can only hope to succeed when he or she understands that a horse being seriously impressive in victory provides no information whatsoever as to whether it will be a good or a bad bet next time out. Elsewhere in this book I've used the word 'impressive' a number of times about a horse I was backing. You'll now understand that this was a form of shorthand, and that I actually meant 'was much more impressive that the experts believed'.

It is sometimes the case that a factor that we know decreases a horse's chance of winning can improve the chance of it being underestimated and hence make it a good betting proposition. You might, for instance, be fairly confident that rain will reduce a horse's chance of winning. But if you believe that this is only probable, whereas the market treats it as almost certain, then you may be justified in placing a bet.

I realise that I may have made life much more difficult for some aspiring punters. Now the bar has been set much higher. Racing is full of experts who have been trained to watch the sport for years. Why should a novice punter have any chance of being able to identify the occasions when the experts have it wrong? The simple answer is that this expertise can only be acquired over time, and that betting will only become a serious business when the necessary skills have been mastered. By realising that you are seeking to back a horse with underestimated factors and bet against a horse with overestimated factors, you will start to acquire the right mindset. By learning to take no interest in betting on factors that are merely positive, i.e. good for a horse's chance of winning, you will start to train your eye in what to look for.

At this point, some may be hoping for a 20-page analysis of which situations tend to lead to horses being under- or overestimated. I could indeed provide a myriad of methods that currently identify horses who fulfil these criteria, but to do so would do no favours to anyone except the bookmakers. It may seem that I am refusing to supply the information that you will need to win, but this entirely misses the point. Look again at my wording: I said that I could provide you with methods that *currently* identify the right horses. Once I'd published such a document, the horses concerned would no longer be underestimated by the market.

As an example, I remember early in my career noticing that David Elsworth's two-year-olds almost never won first time out, even those who later progressed to be top horses. I made the point very strongly on my telephone service, but once I did this the market regarded a win for one of his juvenile debutants as highly unlikely – usually their odds lengthened by the minute. Sure enough, later that year the stable seemed to take advantage of this by preparing one especially to win first time out at good odds. Overestimated had turned full circle to underestimated.

Although providing a list of precise betting criteria would be counterproductive, I shall provide one fully worked example that shows how I was able to progress from starting out as a novice, to noticing how the market was erring, and finally creating a winning method. My example relates to jump racing and it considers how a horse will run on different courses but, in this specific case, the difference is between a sharp course and a testing course.

I'll start by placing you in my shoes at the time I first began analysing racing seriously. I set out knowing nothing about course form, merely being aware that racing took place at a variety of different courses. As I watched and read about racing, I quickly learned that racing experts acknowledged the importance of whether a horse would be suited by a particular course, and that a key part of this was whether a course was sharp or testing.

In my first few seasons, I would watch the Cheltenham Festival with particular interest. I don't imagine I was alone in that, but in what I was doing I may have been. In each race I compared what was expected with what actually happened. I was looking for circumstances that seemed to consistently produce results that were wildly different to expectations. Over the first few years, one trend stood out above others – the market's expectations of horses who had excelled at Kempton's Christmas meeting frequently ended in disappointment at Cheltenham. Time and time again, horses would zip past the line at Kempton only to flop at the festival.

It was a question of trying to identify what had caused that failure. When I did, I noticed that the horses often travelled well but failed to last home. It was clear that stamina seemed to be the issue when Kempton winners went to the Cheltenham Festival. Kempton was a sharp track and Cheltenham was most definitely a testing track. My next job was to research whether this worked out throughout the year, and I kept note of those horses running on testing tracks who had up to that point won only on sharp tracks. Over a large number of meetings, I found that plenty of horses could win at both tracks, and although backing such horses wasn't a profitable strategy, it wasn't a disaster either.

It was a puzzle. Why was I finding that the Cheltenham Festival was more difficult for horses who had excelled on sharp tracks? I reviewed some festival races and pondered the situation carefully, and it became clear that festival races were different to other races at the course. The field tended to race at a much stronger pace from halfway. This was partly due to bigger field sizes, but most likely also caused by the adrenaline flowing through the jockeys at the season's feature meeting. In effect, the closing stages, where horses would quicken and really race against each other at a furious gallop, would start much sooner than races at other Cheltenham meetings. I noticed that in the few festival races where the field was small, say eight runners or fewer, the furious gallop tended to start much later, more in keeping with a normal meeting.

Now I had my answer. In big fields at the festival, the behaviour of the jockeys tended to make the races far more of a test of stamina than the distance would normally demand. I now had the makings of a method. In big fields at Cheltenham I would reinvent the distances to allow for the greater test of stamina. I treated two-mile hurdle races as being two and a quarter miles. I viewed three-mile hurdles as being three miles and three furlongs, and treated the Cheltenham Gold Cup, whose real distance is three miles and two and a half furlongs, as a gruelling three miles and six furlongs. I excluded small fields and also medium-sized fields if I suspected that the early pace would be steady.

From a percentage point of view, this strategy would be the single most effective weapon I used in jump racing. In the Gold Cup itself, I opposed hot favourites with specialist three-mile form and took huge prices each-way about the four-mile plodders who were considered too slow by the pundits. My profit on turnover in the Gold Cup was huge over the years, so much so that even when I gave up jump racing, I maintained my knowledge of the Gold Cup contenders for the next few years and carried on winning. I had a big bet on One Man *not* to win the 1996 Gold Cup, for which he was red-hot favourite. In 1999, I told everyone who asked me that the front two in the betting, Florida Pearl and Teeton Mill, would not last home, and included both the winner See More Business (16-1) and runner-up Go Ballistic (66-1) in my each-way positions. In recent years I have paid much less attention to the jumps, and changes at Cheltenham have made the course a little easier, with faster times. But I still nearly landed a monster win in 2006 on runner-up Hedgehunter, who'd landed the previous year's Grand National. Months before Cheltenham I'd backed Hedgehunter each-way at huge odds and still made a decent profit from the place money.

That, in essence, is how to win at horseracing. You have to develop an expert knowledge of the business. You watch and read and think and notice which situations tend to consistently produce a different result from that expected by the pundits. Then you analyse why they are wrong and develop a strategy that is profit-driven. It's not an easy strategy. You have to pick particular situations where you are better than the experts. As the market is formed by their opinion, it stands to reason that you aren't going to win unless you identify the situations where the experts have it wrong.

The principle of finding the underestimated and beating the experts applies throughout the investment world. Stock-market investors seek to find a company that will surge in value. Many will focus on their liking for the company or product, seemingly unaware that the market price is determined by experts who will have researched the popularity of a company's products over a wide cross-section of the population.

Taking the example of the rise of Starbucks a few years ago, merely knowing that you and your friends liked their coffee shops would have given you no edge over the experts. To obtain an edge over the market, you needed to predict how people's preferences would change in the future. So, a shrewd investor might have spotted the huge popularity of the programme Friends in the mid-1990s. He might have predicted that the public's obsession with a coffee shop-based sitcom might lead to a surge in their desire to frequent coffee shops over the following years. It's essential to stay one step ahead of the experts.

CHAPTER 26

THE FUTURE

PERSONAL profits in excess of £10 million have certainly compensated me for the horrendous period I endured in 1998. I've estimated total bookmaker losses at £20m but this is probably conservative; many of the bets involved turnover hugely greater than my stake, as my agents and their numerous sub-agents all took their share.

It could have been more, but stacking up an unlimited cash pile isn't a priority for me. As I've outlined, I took the year off in 2007 and placed very few bets, making a tiny profit. I returned to working part-time in 2008 and secured a profit just in excess of half a million from a vastly reduced work schedule. These two years have left me feeling very fresh and ready for the coming years in the racing and betting industry.

I have listed the figures in full for the eight years that took me to my profit target of £10m. My profits in 2003 and 2004 were boosted by a side bet with my trading manager Geoffrey Pooley. At the beginning of 2003, I asked him to lay me a bet of £5,000 at evens that I could break the £2m barrier in personal winnings for the season, a bet he accepted. Paradoxically, the bet was an extremely wise financial move on both sides. As a matter of pride, I was determined not to be beaten and worked much harder in the latter stages of 2003 as a result. This cost Geoffrey the £5,000, but his yearly winnings increased dramatically in line with mine. I actually lost the £5,000 back to Geoffrey the following year when I ambitiously set a target of £3m in playing 'double or quits'. I failed, but still set a new personal record of £2.3m.

If the bookmakers want to take heart from the lower profit figures since 2004, they should feel free, as by 2005 I was ready for a sabbatical after many intense years of punting. I had already taken my foot off the pedal. My recent time off has allowed me to develop new strategies. I have an entirely new betting team in place, which will allow me to hide my business better than before. Geoffrey left the business at the end of 2006. He felt that he had won enough to fund new challenges, although he remains involved with me on the ownership side.

Will the bookmakers try even harder to stop me? Not if they have any sense. I've managed well enough so far without having to spend too much time befriending those people in the betting world who have the largest losing accounts. If the layers make my life any more difficult, they will soon find that lots more of their losing punters will become successful after I link up with them. This would be unfortunate for the bookmakers concerned, as they would not only make losses on my bets but also forfeit the future gains from the losing clients when they are forced to make their business less welcome. It's a simple formula. Any bookmaker that fails to act like one will find me joining forces with their best losing clients.

Will my own methods change? Yes, to a certain extent. I've made most of my profits from backing horses at 5-1 or bigger. During my recent time away from betting, I've had plenty of time to consider some new strategies. In the future, I'm sure to be backing plenty of favourites as well, now that terrific value is so readily available on the exchanges. A 5-4 favourite used to work out at 1.06-1 after nine per cent betting tax, whereas these days I'm more likely to be getting 1.46-1 with all these bold new exchange layers keen to give their money away. We'll see what they're made of over the next few years.

The biggest and most controversial change introduced by the birth of exchanges has been the facility for punters to back horses to lose rather than to win. This has created the risk that corrupt partners may seek to profit from ensuring that a horse loses. I am frequently asked if exchanges are a good or bad thing for the integrity of racing. In the long term, I am sure they will prove a good thing, as the computerised audit trail they provide will make it easier to locate wrongdoers.

In the early days of exchanges, the temptation of laying horses for profit proved too much for some professionals involved in racing. It is my view that quite a few jockeys were corrupted at this time and were associating with gamblers who sought to profit by laying their mounts. It is also my view that there were a few jockeys who needed no corrupting and embraced these opportunities with open arms. With a keen ear in the market, I don't think I backed many of the horses who subsequently came under suspicion, but I was the owner of Polar Kingdom, who was found to have been advised as a likely loser by his jockey on two days when I had backed it. Hmmm.

Although the efforts of the racing authorities and, latterly, the City of London police have not been as successful in as many cases as they hoped, I am confident that the whole business has sent a shockwave through those in racing who sought to profit from breaking the rules. I have no doubt that corruption will still occur, but I am far more confident about the integrity of racing than I was five years ago.

If racing is going to be kept free of corruption, the rules need to be tight on both sides of the fence. On a general point, bookmakers' public relations officers (PROs), I believe should avoid contact with jockeys. The authorities should also have acted when former PRO Ron Pollard published a book called *Odds and Sods*, in which he admitted that years earlier he had been involved in paying off jockeys on behalf of bookmaker William Hill, who founded the modern bookmaking chain. Fixing races is fixing races. I don't care how long ago it was done.

I wish the best of luck to those in the betting industry who seem hell-bent on trying to predict what I might back and jump in front of me. After Exponential won in 2004, there have been an incredible number of mythical gambles on Stuart Williams-trained horses, and now probably the best laying system in racing, for those who want to play bookmaker, is to lay all horses trained by Stuart. Anybody following this system over the last couple of years would have shown a huge profit. The market and the press have managed to convince themselves that every horse the stable runs is a potential gamble. Unfortunately, as an owner in the yard, I'm not allowed to lay the stable's horses, so I can offer up this method for free.

I'm sure that my ownership interests will continue to flourish. Having had two Royal Ascot winners in four years, I'm already finding that one or two substantial investors are approaching me with a view to becoming involved. My ability to spot a quality horse early in its career is a huge asset, and I suspect that over the coming years my operation may compete at an even higher level. This would allow me to use my expertise without the endless toil of studying low-grade handicaps.

I offer one last reminder to aspiring gamblers. Before you have a bet, make sure you examine all the evidence available to you, not just the easy parts of the equation. Different factions tend to focus on their own sections of the sport. If a horse wins impressively watched by a mixed group, the trainer will first note who trained it, the jockey will wonder who rode it, a breeder will point to the successful sire, and the punter will ask whether it was well backed. A true professional will assess all aspects in seeking out the underestimated.

My life, in general, has turned out better than I could ever have dreamed. Certainly, betting professionally was the best decision I've ever made. However, I accept that betting, though highly profitable, is a slightly frivolous way to spend my time, so over the years I'm sure I'll diversify, although the bookmakers will need to pay me out many more millions before I'm finished with them.

From a moral point of view, I feel entirely comfortable, as my winnings are derived by reducing the profits of the major betting corporations, but in time I may also seek some more productive uses of my mind. Although it wasn't always easy along the way, I'm now fortunate to live the life I do, and at some stage will certainly aim to do something more useful to society than relieving the big bookmakers of some of their profits. I have a friend who is a magistrate, and that is an avenue I may explore in later life.

But it all comes back to 1998. I wouldn't have achieved half as much if I hadn't been spurred on by what happened to me that terrifying evening in June. I still retain some of the old habits that were necessary during my months in hiding, for example I continue to automatically carefully check any car that pulls alongside me as I walk down the pavement. It's just a habit from my former life. Just in case, I still retain my police connections.

There's an expression to the effect that it's better to travel than to arrive. A friend asked me not long ago whether, given my time again, I'd choose to go through that first 12 months once more if I knew where I'd end up ten years later. I turned and looked in horror at him. "No," I replied, before a long pause. "And not for ten times the amount." In my case, it has definitely been better to arrive than to travel.

A full analysis of the eight years it took to reach my profit target.

1999	+ £814,935.70
2000	+ £1,152,436.34
2001	+ £579,761.71
2002	+ £1,341,185.54

2003	+ £2,180,907.05
2004	+ £2,339,282.99
2005	+ £569,147.24
2006	+ £1,072,326.46
Grand Total:	**+£10,049,983.03**

GLOSSARY

All-weather racing Generally low-grade action staged on an artificial surface

Ante-post Relating to betting on a race before the day it is run

Apprentice Inexperienced jockey who receives a weight allowance (7lb, 5lb, 3lb) from senior riders

At The Races One of the two satellite TV channels (the other being Racing UK) that broadcast from all British racecourses

Betfair Internet betting exchange, in which punters bet with each other rather than a bookmaker

Betting tax Now obsolete, a percentage payable on bets in betting shops at time of placing or at time of collection. For much of its use until its removal in 2001, tax was nine per cent.

BHA British Horseracing Association, racing's rulers

Blinkers, eyeshield, visor Equipment worn by a horse to aid concentration

Breeze-up Sale for horses in the spring of their two-year-old careers where they cover a distance at racing pace (are breezed) before being sold

Claimer Usually low-grade affair in which any horse can be claimed for a price set and published pre-race

Draw bias Situation where the ground on one side of a racecourse is faster than on the other side, whether through artificial watering or track topography, and thus horses in stalls (drawn) on that side are deemed to be favoured

Goffs Irish sales company

Group 1 race Flat race of the highest quality, eg Derby, 2,000 Guineas, July Cup, King George; followed by Group 2 and Group 3 levels

Handicap mark   Rating allotted to all horses by the official handi-capper as a benchmark of ability

Jackpot   Tote permutation bet that requires punters to select a horse to win each of six races at a meeting

Knavesmire   Historical name for York racecourse

Listed race   Race straddling the divide between Group 1, 2 and 3 races and handicaps

Maiden   Race for horses who have yet to win

Nursery   Handicap race for two-year-olds

Penalty   Extra weight allotted for a given race if horse concerned is successful after the weights for that race have been framed

Placepot   Tote permutation bet that requires punters to select a horse to be placed in each of six races at a meeting

Point-to-Point   Amateur jump racing

Pricewise   A column in the *Racing Post* that highlights horses con-sidered to overpriced in the morning betting

Racing UK   One of the two satellite TV channels (the other being At The Races) that broadcast from all British racecourses

Rails   As in rails bookmaker, an individual or firm at a race meet-ing that stands at the rail dividing Members and Tattersalls and takes larger bets than the rest of the Tattersalls bookmakers

Reverse forecast   To combine two horses in a bet that pays out whether A finishes second to B or B finishes second to A

Scoop6   Tote permutation bet that requires punters to select the winners of six previously determined races on any given Saturday

Seller   Low-quality race in which the winner is sold at auction immediately afterwards

SP   Starting Price

Talking horse   Horse whose ability rests on reputation rather than deeds

Tattersalls   British sales company based in Newmarket

The Morning Line   Saturday morning Channel 4 programme devoted to racing

The Sporting Life   Racing daily with a wide orbit of fame until it was closed down in May 1998

Timeform   Firm of form and ratings experts

Tote, William Hill, Ladbrokes, Coral, Betfred   Major bookmaking chains in Britain

Union Jack   'Exotic' bet involving nine horses in various combinations

Yankee   'Exotic' bet involving four horses in various combinations

INDEX

258